Dearest Patricia,

Mahalo for all
your inspiration & support!

♡ Noela

21ST CENTURY INVESTING

21ST CENTURY INVESTING

INVESTING

Redirecting Financial Strategies
to Drive Systems Change

**William Burckart
and Steve Lydenberg**

Berrett–Koehler Publishers, Inc.

Berrett-Koehler Publishers, Inc.
1333 Broadway, Suite 1000
Oakland, CA 94612-1921
Tel: (510) 817-2277
Fax: (510) 817-2278
www.bkconnection.com

ORDERING INFORMATION

Quantity sales. Special discounts are available on quantity purchases by corporations, associations, and others. For details, contact the "Special Sales Department" at the Berrett-Koehler address above.

Individual sales. Berrett-Koehler publications are available through most bookstores. They can also be ordered directly from Berrett-Koehler: Tel: (800) 929-2929; Fax: (802) 864-7626; www.bkconnection.com.

Orders for college textbook / course adoption use. Please contact Berrett-Koehler: Tel: (800) 929-2929; Fax: (802) 864-7626.

Distributed to the US trade and internationally by Penguin Random House Publisher Services.

Berrett-Koehler and the BK logo are registered trademarks of Berrett-Koehler Publishers, Inc.

Printed in the United States.

Berrett-Koehler books are printed on long-lasting acid-free paper. When it is available, we choose paper that has been manufactured by environmentally responsible processes. These may include using trees grown in sustainable forests, incorporating recycled paper, minimizing chlorine in bleaching, or recycling the energy produced at the paper mill.

Library of Congress Cataloging-in-Publication Data

Names: Burckart, William, author. | Lydenberg, Steven D., author.
Title: 21st century investing : redirecting financial strategies to drive systems change / William Burckart and Steve Lydenberg.
Description: 1st Edition. | Oakland : Berrett-Koehler Publishers, 2021. Includes bibliographical references and index.
Identifiers: LCCN 2020051901 | ISBN 9781523091072 (hardcover) | ISBN 9781523091089 (adobe pdf) | ISBN 9781523091096 (epub)
Subjects: LCSH: Investments. | Stocks. | Social responsibility of business.
Classification: LCC HG4521 .B7877 2021 | DDC 332.6--dc23
LC record available at https://lccn.loc.gov/2020051901

First Edition
26 25 24 23 22 21   10 9 8 7 6 5 4 3 2 1

Text designer: Marin Bookworks
Cover designer: Annica Lydenberg
Editor: PeopleSpeak

For Penelope and Theodore,
Annica and Jackson,
and Jack

Contents

Preface..ix

Introduction   There's No Time to Lose..1

Chapter One   Set Goals..23

Chapter Two   Decide Where to Focus...41

Chapter Three   Allocate Assets...53

Chapter Four   Apply Investment Tools...71

Chapter Five   Leverage Advanced Techniques.........................87

Chapter Six   Evaluate Results..113

Chapter Seven   Case Example: Investing to Address

                             Income Inequality..129

Chapter Eight   Investors in Transition..149

Conclusion   The Time to Act Is Now......................................169

Notes..175

Acknowledgments..197

Index...203

About the Authors...215

Preface

IT'S TIME for a new way to think about investing, one that can contend with the complex challenges we face in the 21st century.

Investment today has evolved historically from a basic, conventional approach (concern about the risks of security selection and portfolio risk management) to embrace as well sustainable investment (intentionally achieving social and environmental benefits along with financial returns). Building on this integration of sustainability factors, it can now transition to a third stage that recognizes both the power of investments to impact social, financial, and environmental systems and the complexity of the times we live in. We call this *system-level investing*.

System-level investors believe that it is time to support and enhance the health and stability of the social, financial, and environmental systems on which they depend for long-term returns. They preserve and strengthen these fundamental systems while still generating competitive or otherwise acceptable performance.

This book is for those investors who believe in that transition. They may be institutions, large or small, concerned about the long-term stability of the environment and society. They may be individual investors who want their children and grandchildren to inherit a just and sustainable world. They may have already adopted sustainable investment strategies and be ready to transition to system-level investment. Or they may never have considered alternatives to a conventional approach.

Whoever they may be, they will find the what, why, and how of this transition in these pages: *what* it means to manage system-level risks and rewards, *why* it is imperative to do so now, and *how* to integrate this new way of thinking into their current practice. In particular, the book provides investors with a process for setting goals, deciding where to focus, allocating assets, applying investment tools, leveraging advanced techniques, and evaluating results. It helps investors build on their current practice and, by incorporating system-level perspectives, better align the investments of today with society's long-term goals.

When we say *systems*, we are talking about those large social, financial, and environmental foundations of society necessary for any successful investment. At the broadest levels, social systems include healthcare, food and water security, fair employment, freedom of expression, consumer safety, economic and environmental justice, and education and training. Financial systems include fair and honest markets, access to basic services, and transparency of data. Global environmental systems include climate stability, natural resources, oceans and fresh water, forests, and arable land. These large systems are in turn made up of subsystems. All are interconnected and ultimately impact one another.

Understanding these systems—and ensuring their resilience—is more important than ever. Because we live in an increasingly populated, complex, and interconnected world, a disruption in one can cause multiple others to fall like dominos in a line.

When we refer to *investing*, we include finance in all its forms (stocks, bonds, real estate, venture capital, and lending of various sorts, among others) and styles (growth, value, emerging markets, large or small scale, and the like). We are talking about Investment with a capital *I*.

When we refer to *system-level investors*, we could be referring to all investors because all investments have impacts and implications for social, financial, or environmental systems. We use the term here more narrowly, however. We mean those who intentionally set out to manage their impacts on the largest, most important global systems. They deliberately adopt investment strategies that seek to minimize systemic risks at these levels and promote opportunities for system-wide rewards.

Some in the investment community today have already set off down the road to a genuinely system-oriented approach, but few are yet fully committed. Those making progress adopt tactics such as investing in portfolios entirely targeted or heavily weighted toward social and environmental solutions and advocate for public policies that reduce systemic risks and advance the health and resilience of crucial systems. They engage at industry levels to set standards and norms. They collaborate with others to amplify their influence. And they set clear goals for system-level (not simply portfolio-related) progress and report on their contributions to the achievement of these goals.

It is now time for a new era of investing with a vision that expands beyond individual returns and beating the performance of your neighbor. Most people don't trust Wall Street anymore.

The "greed is good" mantra rings false. And there is a burgeoning interest among a wide range of investors in generating positive social and environmental returns along with profits.

By calling this approach *system-level investing*, we want to be clear: a primary responsibility of 21st century investors—whether individuals, families, or institutions—is to ensure that their investments intentionally support the health and resilience of crucial systems, reduce systemic risks, and promote opportunities for all.

Doing so is not only what investment should be but what it must be if the financial community is to do its part to avoid a multiplicity of collapses and crises that will threaten our complex world in the coming decades.

Today, investors of all sorts have the opportunity to become part of this important transition and early adopters of a flagship movement.

There's No Time to Lose

WHAT ARE the biggest threats to an investor's portfolio these days?

Income inequality is stirring nationalistic protectionist rage, upending democracies, and prompting trade wars. Pandemics are shutting down economies and draining local governments of the funds to support workers, communities, and businesses. Risk takers looking for fast returns brought the financial system to near collapse, triggering massive unemployment and government bailouts. Disparities in gender and racial diversity and inclusion are hampering economic growth and fracturing social cohesion. Attempts to preserve fossil-fuel jobs are slowing progress toward a low-carbon economy, worsening climate change, which in turn accelerates droughts that then lead to the mass migrations that threaten yet more jobs.

These are the 21st century's fundamentally destabilizing, new and different, social and environmental challenges. They are global. They have tipping points that once passed cannot be reversed. They are systemic risks in a highly interconnected and complex world. And they threaten long-term investment returns across all asset classes in ways that traditional risk management cannot cope with.

Yet *conventional investors* continue to invest as usual, ignoring massively destabilizing challenges and giving little thought to the contributions they make to them. Instead, situations get worse as they rack up short-term profits. They view sustainability and environmental, social, and governance (ESG) factors with suspicion. They believe that they will lose money if they go down that road and that this way of investing is no more than a passing fad. When it comes to all things social and environmental, if the government hasn't told them not to do it, they can do whatever they please; and anyhow, whatever they do doesn't really change anything.

As a result, they declare sustainability and ESG irrelevant. Their primary goal is to maximize returns in as short a time as possible without consideration of such issues. They diversify. They hedge. They look for the next new thing, but they don't see polar ice caps melting and the poor getting poorer and rich richer. They pat themselves on the back thinking they are doing their job. When asked why they don't do anything about systemic crises, they say, "My job is to make money; someone else needs to deal with the systemic challenges of this world."

Sustainable investors have a different take. They recognize the positive social and environmental impacts that specific investments have and intentionally integrate such holdings into their portfolios. They seek ESG benefits along with their financial returns. They invest in an affordable housing project here, a wind power company there. Their portfolios don't include tobacco producers or maybe even coal mining firms. They ask this company to disclose more data on diversity or that one to improve its safety standards at a supplier overseas.

They represent progress. They see the social and environmental challenges in the world and try to keep their portfolios fair and clean. They think allocating assets to strong ESG performers while generating competitive returns is a worthwhile activity. But how can they get beyond fair and clean portfolios to a changed system? How do they propose to make a difference that lasts? While sustainable investment helps investors to manage ESG impacts in their portfolios, it stops short of helping manage systemic challenges. It runs the risk of missing the forest for the trees. In thinking about climate change, a sustainable investor may look at a portfolio of solar power companies and congratulate himself because it is clean. But what if the rest of the world just goes on generating even more greenhouse gas emissions? When asked why he didn't do more, he says, "I did my part; that's all I can do."

Examples of Three Approaches to System-Level Investing

A growing class of investors—we call them *system-level investors*—acknowledges that they have an impact, whether negative or positive, on the global social, financial, and environmental systems and that those systemic challenges impact their portfolios in return. These investors intentionally manage the risks and rewards at these levels to provide a stable, resilient foundation for investments across all their asset classes. They set explicit goals for their impact on systems, use a range of techniques to reach those goals, and measure their progress toward them. They seek to preserve and enhance foundational social, financial, and

3

environmental systems in the long term while achieving competitive returns.

Applying a System-Level Lens to Address Income Inequality

Let's consider the example of income inequality. This is one of the most difficult issues for conventional investors to confront because they benefit from it themselves. Their stocks go up. Their compensation does too. They like companies that cut labor costs, that avoid paying taxes when they can. They don't invest in government bonds when they see higher returns in private markets.

Sustainable investors, by contrast, see the challenge. They don't ignore what's there. So they ask a large company they've invested in to up its minimum wage. They add bonds supporting low-income housing to their fixed-income portfolios. They vote against a company's board that still doesn't have women on it. They won't invest in a company that recently had a major safety accident at an overseas facility. They clean up their holdings. They are making progress, but is the world around them changing for the better? Are they asking how they can contribute to fundamental change? Or is that just a step too far?

System-level investors ask not only what they can do for this or that portfolio but what initiatives they can take that will create fundamental change in a system that has generated growing income inequality. That is, how can they lessen the problem of income inequality itself and reduce instability in the system while enriching the universe of prospects in which they might invest and create a rising tide of opportunities for all?

They look for leverage points within the current system that will drive change. This means, for example, advocating for a minimum wage not just by one firm but in a locality, state, or nation. The same can be said for other key leverage points such as diversity, unions and workers' rights, taxes, and safety: these investors want to see to it that industry standards are set—voluntary if necessary, regulatory if possible—and demand that the government enforce the laws and regulations already on the books.

They recognize that to make system-level change happen, one voice alone is not enough. System-level investors join with their peers to amplify their message on the importance of addressing income inequality and increase their influence. How else can they control the systemic risks that income inequality now poses and create the investment opportunities they need? How else are they going to keep from making income inequality worse?

Applying a System-Level Lens to Improve Healthcare

Next we'll look at investors inspired to contend with the systemic risks and challenges of our current healthcare system and not just with seeking to profit from it in its current form. They might be endowments of hospitals or healthcare-related foundations or the asset managers for life insurance companies with a vested interest in the maintenance of an effective and smoothly functioning system. Or they could simply be individuals concerned about the inability of today's system to ensure affordable care for one and all.

Conventional investors will not pay much attention to social challenges and affordability. They will study changing demographics, trends in epidemiology, technological innovations, and the pipeline of new drugs pharmaceutical companies are bringing to the market—all with an eye to picking stocks. Whether people can afford to stay healthy and whether the population is getting sicker or healthier are not among their concerns. Others can worry about such questions while they tend to their returns.

For their portfolios, sustainable investors search out technology companies that reduce healthcare costs, pharmaceutical companies seeking cures for neglected diseases in developing countries, and generic drug companies serving the developing world with low-cost business models. They avoid companies with histories of product quality controversies or fraud. They ask for more data on the pricing policies of those marketing patent-protected drugs. They urge companies to improve their rankings on the Access to Medicine Index, which ranks twenty of the world's largest pharmaceutical companies based on their efforts to address access to medicine. The larger problem of whether overall health outcomes are improving or not is nevertheless not directly on their radar.

But system-level investors will translate their interest into action differently. They integrate into their practice guiding principles such as those of a globally respected healthcare standard setter—say, the World Health Organization. They create portfolios with holdings that embody a healthcare system with widely accepted characteristics such as affordability, efficiency, reliability, trustworthiness, and accessibility. They invest in widely accepted healthy living practices like preventative medicine, healthy diets, and exercise. Their fixed-income portfolios include the debt of nonprofit hospitals and community healthcare groups. Their venture capital investments include drug companies specializing in vaccines.

They engage with key stakeholders in the system—the corporations that are incurring healthcare insurance costs that put them at a competitive disadvantage, the hospitals that are struggling to contain drug costs, their peers in the investment industry that are still looking for short-term opportunities in the sector rather than contending with the costs to the nation's economy of the overall system—to identify best practices that will lead to better outcomes for all. They encourage communications and trust among these stakeholders and work to establish best practices and pressure regulatory change that will set a level playing field. They understand the political nature of the healthcare insurance debate and engage with the healthcare industry and legislators to work toward consensus on best practices.

Applying a System-Level Lens to Combat Climate Change

More and more, investors have woken up to the reality of climate change. They recognize the huge challenges that climate change already poses. Conventional investors, though, view the emerging crises as an investment opportunity, not as a threat that needs to be addressed as rapidly as possible. They may consider investment opportunities that melting ice sheets will open up for drilling for oil in the Arctic or mining metals in Greenland, that mass migrations will create for building fences between countries, that droughts will generate for desalination companies—at the same time that they look for the next hot stock in the renewable energy field.

Sustainable investors, instead, concentrate on keeping their portfolios clean. They may divest from fossil-fuel companies partially (coal only) or entirely (oil, natural gas, refineries, and oil-field services companies too). They will add wind and solar power firms as well. They may also look for companies that market energy-efficient products (appliances and air conditioners) or have energy-efficiency programs in place. They will engage with any bad actors left in their portfolios to get them to reduce their carbon dioxide emissions or improve the energy usage of their products.

System-level investors, however, are not satisfied with various holdings that tell a climate-positive story or engagement with a few companies to up their use of renewable energy. Instead, they look to build a portfolio of companies devoted to solar energy, wind power, battery storage, next-generation energy efficiency, sustainable forest products, regenerative agriculture, and the like that can provide a holistic vision of what an alternative world could be.

They do not stop there but participate in calls for mandatory disclosure on greenhouse gas (GHG) emissions so they can make intelligent investment decisions; join with their peers in global collaborative efforts like Climate Action 100+, with its five-year engagement strategy to reduce the GHG emissions of the 161 most systematically important emitters around the world; create new markets for climate-friendly investment products like "green bonds" and support the setting of voluntary and government-backed standards for what defines those markets; urge trade associations not to work against their members' calls for climate action; and support regulatory measures that promote the development of climate-friendly industries through subsidies, tax abatements, preferential purchasing programs, carbon pricing or taxes, and the like. They look for leverage points within systems that can catalyze change. They set goals at a system level and measure their progress toward those goals.

The investment world is evolving rapidly. The lines between conventional, sustainable, and system-level investing often blur. Conventional investors may launch a sustainable product here and there. Sustainable investors use this or that system-level technique. Whole firms are even transitioning from one level to another. Nevertheless, the three approaches are distinct, and we use these distinctions to clarify the range of approaches available. For conventional investors, no consideration is given to ESG factors. For sustainable investors, ESG factors are considered as to their short-term financial materiality, and both financial and social and environmental benefits are sought. For system-level investors, an additional concern is added: their impact on the long-term health of the social, financial, and environmental systems on which their investments ultimately depend.

Systems Are Important, *Really* Important

Many investors increasingly understand that the two objectives of making money and solving global challenges are not just compatible but synergistic. And so do we. Just as modern portfolio theory (MPT)—today's dominant investment paradigm— extended analysis of individual stocks to a basket of securities (that is, portfolios), a system-level approach helps investors to move their level of analysis beyond just portfolios to include the context (that is, the systems) in which these portfolios exist.[1]

Finance and investment are built on the predictability and reliability of society, the financial system, and the environment. These systems are important, *really* important. Stable systems promote healthy markets; unstable systems lead to reduced or negative market returns. And the decisions made daily by investors—institutions and individuals—impact the fate of these systems inevitably and powerfully whether these investors recognize that or not.

Standing today between investors and their ability to understand that their portfolio-level decisions can collectively create system-level obstacles that undermine their long-term returns are a number of ingrained habits and beliefs. First, managers— like their corporate executive peers—are told that their duty is to generate the greatest returns in the shortest time possible; the invisible hand of the market will then guide their efficient actions to the best outcome for society. This philosophy has led to an increasing short-termism in the markets with its emphasis on shareholder primacy, which has in turn led to rising inequalities around the world.

Fortifying the health of the systems that underlie the market is actually the greatest source of overall absolute performance for investors. James Hawley and Jon Lukomnik, for example, point out that investors' focus on outperformance of the market—that is, creating "alpha"—misses the point: investors on the whole benefit from the performance of the overall market, driven in large part by the performance of the economy. They say:

> Contrary to theory, investors can and do affect overall market risk and return. Indeed . . . they should seek to do so.

However, the idea that investing is atomistic—that is, portfolio investment takes place within the context of systemic market risk and return, and is affected by it but is unable to affect it—is ingrained in the asset management industry as it is in MPT itself, in spite of the variety of MPT versions that have evolved since the 1950s.

The irony is that more than 90 percent of the variation of return an investor will receive is explained by the return from the risk profile of the universe of securities they are invested in and not by the stock selection undertaken by the asset manager.[2]

These "market beta" swings in benchmark indexes against which investors' performance is measured are the primary source of long-term returns, rather than the alpha that individual investors generate by outperforming those benchmarks.

The decisions of investors as market participants affect the economy as a whole, drive benchmark indexes up and down, and, when it comes to their social and environmental impacts, can tip the scales toward either crises or stability. Investors need to understand the relationship between their actions and the health of the social, financial, and environmental systems that they depend on for financial success. These are system-level risks and rewards and require system-level solutions.

Fortunately, the investment community is not helpless in the face of this uncertain future. It has the power to make societies, markets, and the environment resilient and to prepare for the challenges of the 21st century. But a new way of thinking about how to make investment serve these purposes is needed—an approach that balances returns in the marketplace with benefits for society.

There Is a Solution: System-Level Investing

System-level investing challenges investors to think beyond price alone. Its job is not done by simply creating a portfolio with some social or environmental benefits. It takes investors beyond asking What are the carbon emissions and working-condition consequences of our investment in this enterprise or that fund? In addition, they want to know What can we do to minimize the risks of climate change globally and prevent abusive labor throughout all supply chains? How can we add meaningfully to poverty alleviation and an empowered and diverse workforce?

This transition from conventional and sustainable investing to system-level investing may require a conceptual leap. But investment has always changed with the times, and now it's time to change again.

Two decades into the 21st century, investors have begun to make progress toward a system-level approach. It is common sense that investment must evolve with the times, building on past gains to account for the changes of today. As one advisor once asked us, "If you went to a cardiologist who said you needed heart surgery and they were going to do it the same way they did it in the 1950s, what would you do?" You'd look for another doctor. Stat.

Conventional investors have taken initial steps down this road. Considering the impacts of technological disruptions or political risks is not all that different from understanding how macro trends such as climate change or social unrest can affect portfolio performance. Indeed, these factors often overlap, as, for example, when the National Intelligence Council reported that

water risk in Southeast Asia will contribute to the risk of instability and state failure in the future.[3] Similarly, considerations
of corporations' stakeholder relations often center around large
societal issues such as human rights, treatment of employees,
workplace or community health and safety, income inequality,
and the like. Investors already factoring quality of management
into their financial analyses are halfway to understanding how
these issues can directly affect specific securities and to asking
whether on a system-wide level these considerations have relevant implications.[4]

Sustainable investors, too, have made headway in a transition toward system-level considerations, as we explore further
in chapter 8.

Self-identified "universal owners" such as Japan's Government
Pension Investment Fund, with its $1.7 trillion in assets under
management, invest in a cross-section of securities in virtually
all asset classes. They recognize that because they "own" the
economy, their success is bound up with the health and prosperity of that economy as a whole and have begun to act on that
recognition.

Investors with long-term time horizons such as Norges Bank
Investment Management recognize that the further out they
look, the more their interests and those of society coincide. The
greater their commitment to a long-term approach, the more
they value the health of underlying systems.

The Church of England Pensions Board believes that a range
of "stewardship responsibilities" including ESG matters is
essential to its long-term fiduciary duties and obligations. The
practice of stewardship acknowledges investors' ownership

obligations to consider the financial implications of practices with broad societal implications, thereby transcending the conventional "financial only" view implicit in conventional market-based buy-and-sell disciplines.[5]

Self-identified impact investors such as the KL Felicitas Foundation intentionally seek to generate social and environmental benefit through their investments along with financial returns. In addition, as part of their commitment to essentially "bet the farm" on impact investing, Felicitas has extended its mission to enabling the global financial system to achieve greater social and environmental impact.[6]

These are among the investors making a transition to a system-level approach in its varied forms today. They have come a long way from the often-repeated conventional wisdom that social and environmental issues have no place in investment. And in doing so, they have laid the foundation for a fully articulated systemic approach, one that pushes an entire social or environmental system to a fundamental reset of its mindset, creating increased benefits for society and opportunities for all investors.

This systemic approach means investing in portfolios entirely targeted or heavily weighted toward not just mitigating social and environmental issues but actually solving them. It also means advocating for public policies that reduce systemic risks and advance the health and resilience of crucial systems. Investors focused on systems are engaging at industry levels to set standards and norms. In addition, they are collaborating with others to amplify investors' influence. And they are reporting on investors' contributions to the achievement of these goals.

Investors Sparked a Movement; We're Helping Fan the Flame

This book shows how investors can now integrate and extend current practice to include a system-oriented focus. All investors—including individuals, families, local institutions, and large pension funds and financial services firms—can pursue this path. The essential steps of the process are laid out in chapters 1 through 6. Although we primarily use examples from institutional investors to illustrate the specifics, we also point to lessons learned that individuals can integrate into their own practice. For example, they can ask their financial advisors to urge their money managers to adopt the specific steps toward system-level investing outlined in the subsequent chapters.

The fundamental idea behind this book grew from our previous work in the fields of sustainable and impact investment. Lydenberg was an early pioneer of the sustainable investment movement and has been consistently pushing the field forward over the course of four decades. Burckart began in the early 2000s in venture philanthropy and moved toward impact investing only in 2008—the one following the other by about three decades.

Soon after we met in 2014, we agreed that the financial world stood at a tipping point from which it could move beyond a portfolio focus to a focus on entire systems. To move the investment community down this road, we formed The Investment Integration Project (TIIP), an applied research and consulting services firm, to do just that: to help investors understand the big-picture context of their investments.[7] It was an ambitious endeavor led by a septuagenarian and millennial who can look backward, learning from the advancements the investing world has already made, and forward, toward the increasingly complex world of interlocking social and environmental systems.

We coined the term *system-level investing* and started helping institutional investors understand the feedback loops between their investments and these overarching systems. This has meant nudging them to fundamentally rethink their mission and to use a more diverse set of tools. Sudden shocks to our financial and economic systems such as the pandemic of 2020 and the steady and persistent destabilization of our environment by climate change have made illustrating the need for this change a lot easier.[8]

The obstacles to a world where investors seek to improve the resilience of systems, although substantial, are not insurmountable. The first step is the recognition that all investments have impacts beyond the portfolio. As Mark Carney, the former governor of the Bank of England, forcefully put it, "We need to recognize the tension between pure free market capitalism, which reinforces the primacy of the individual at the expense of the system, and social capital which requires from individuals a broader sense of responsibility for the system. A sense of self must be accompanied by a sense of the systemic."[9]

This Book Gives Investors a Road Map

Once investors have taken that initial step, other adjustments in the investment process follow inevitably. This book summarizes the frameworks we've developed through TIIP to illustrate that process, how it relates to conventional and sustainable investment, and why it can usher in a new way of thinking about investment. Table 1 summarizes the road map to incorporating system-level investing. This journey begins with a willingness to build on and extend the best practices from conventional and sustainable investment to embrace the contexts of the social and environmental systems within which they operate.

Table 1. Steps in the process

Process	Conventional		Sustainable		System-Level
Set goals	Create efficient portfolios that maximize returns and therefore benefit society.	&	Create portfolios that also address social and environmental challenges and therefore add a second level of value.	&	Influence social and environmental systems to generate positive impacts from the outset and therefore benefit all investors' returns in the long run (chapter 1).
Decide where to focus	Select managers and styles. Decide on market risks to be taken.	&	Focus on specific social and environmental challenges pertinent to investment. Choose securities and financial instruments that address those challenges.	&	Identify a social or environmental systemic challenge impacting all asset classes. Justify the choice by assessing consensus, relevance, effectiveness, and uncertainty involved (chapter 2).
Allocate assets	Consider historical risks and financial performance of specific asset classes.	&	Consider the ability of specific securities to generate social and environmental rewards.	&	Consider the ability of specific asset classes to create systemic social and environmental benefits (chapter 3).

Table 1 (continued)

Process	Conventional		Sustainable		System-Level
Apply investment tools	Use investment beliefs statement to formalize convictions about whether markets are efficient and whether risk is rewarded in the marketplace. Avoid (favor) overvalued (undervalued) securities. Sell poorly performing securities or engage on business strategies.	&	State beliefs about ESG benefits and impact on valuation. Target sustainability themes. Avoid (favor) holdings with weak (strong) sustainability impacts. Engage with holdings to improve social and environmental performance.	&	State beliefs about the benefits of healthy social and environmental systems. Invest to solve systemic challenges. Apply social and environmental standards and engage to establish system-wide norms (chapter 4).
Leverage advanced techniques	Incorporate economic and political macro trends into investment strategy.	&	Align portfolios with broadly accepted social and environmental goals such as the UN Sustainable Development Goals.	&	Use tools designed specifically to manage systemic risks and rewards: field building, investment enhancement, and opportunity generation (chapter 5).
Evaluate results	Report portfolios' financial performance versus established benchmarks. Assess managers' contribution to portfolios' performance.	&	Report portfolios' contribution to addressing social and environmental challenges. Provide details of the what, how much, who, nature, and risks of those contributions.	&	In relationship to systemic influence, assess managers' consistency of beliefs and actions, choice of tools, effectiveness of their application, success in aligning interests among systems' stakeholders, and contribution to progress toward systems that generate desirable outcomes from the outset (chapter 6).

The six key elements of that process are the same for all investors: set goals, decide where to focus, allocate assets, apply investment tools, leverage advanced techniques, and evaluate results. For each step along the way we illustrate the need for and benefits of incorporating a system-level perspective. This 21st century investment discipline puts a powerful tool for change in investors' hands. It requires a balancing of multiple considerations, which may at first appear burdensome. But the need for balance is already inherent in conventional and sustainable investment: balancing risk and reward, income and asset appreciation, social benefit and financial returns, public good or harm and private gain. Such balancing acts may not be easy, but that simply means that managers must sharpen and demonstrate their skills.

Each chapter of the book positions this system-level approach in the context of conventional and sustainable investment practices as they have evolved and provides examples of how investors can put this new perspective into action.

Chapter 1 describes why setting system-level investment goals is essential. It examines the current status, strengths, and limitations of conventional, sustainable, and system-level investments—their goals and underlying assumptions.

Chapter 2 describes the first crucial step for system-level investors: choosing an issue on which to focus and justifying that choice. The key elements in that justification are consensus, relevance, effectiveness, and uncertainty.

Chapter 3 focuses on asset allocation and takes an in-depth look at how system-level investors can make decisions about what asset classes to emphasize and how that choice can enhance the social and environmental impacts that various asset classes are designed to achieve.

Chapter 4 identifies how to apply system-level thinking to conventional investing tools. It shows how system-level investors can take familiar tools—investment policy and beliefs statements, disciplines for security selection, engagement with portfolio holdings, and selection of managers—and extend their use to encompass system-level perspectives. This chapter portrays the logical extension of today's conventional and sustainability tools to the realm of systemic influence and risk management.

Chapter 5 explores the unconventional techniques that investors can leverage to help establish a system-level perspective. They include field building (self-organization, interconnectedness, and polity), investment enhancement (standards setting, solutions, and diversity of approaches), and opportunity generation (additionality, evaluations, locality, and utility).

Chapter 6 proposes a system-level measurement and reporting framework to facilitate the widespread adoption of system-level investing. It explores how prevailing outputs-focused approaches to measurement and reporting are too narrowly focused and fall short. Instead, it advocates for an approach to measurement and reporting that is more comprehensive and assesses the roles of investors and their actions, along with the outcomes of these actions.

Chapter 7 provides a practical example of how investors can address one of the most challenging systemic risks of our time: income inequality. It points out that some of the steps necessary to address this issue are difficult for investors to contend with within the current conventional framework: labor, taxes, and compensation in the corporate and financial worlds.

Chapter 8 includes six portraits of investors on the road to system-level investment through universal ownership, steward-ship, long-term value creation, impact investment, ESG integra-tion, and standards setting. It also presents three scenarios that show how these building blocks have laid the foundation for the logical next steps on the road to a systemic perspective.

We conclude the book with our vision of what a world would look like in which investors of all types, institutions and individ-uals, incorporated system-level perspectives into their approach and practice—and call out the next steps that those motivated to follow this path can easily take as they start their journey.

CHAPTER ONE

Set Goals

LEO TOLSTOY, the famed Russian writer, penned a fairy tale in 1899 called *The Big Oven* that feels very prescient for today. The story is about a man who has a large oven to heat his large home, though only he and his wife live there. He starts to run out of firewood in the worsening Russian winter. Ignoring the suggestions of neighbors to conserve by getting a smaller oven, he instead feeds it all the wood available to him, including the wood from his fences, his roof, and his ceiling. He eventually tears down his whole home in a vain attempt to keep it heated and has to ultimately go live with strangers—all because he was unwilling to face the fundamental problem and actually fix it, settling for short-term band-aids instead of a cure.[1]

We've heard that we're "burning down the house" by under-reacting to climate change, and the same could be said for the finance industry. We've already seen how a myopic focus on the here and now has hurt us—how the oven of investors' focus on maximizing short-term returns is burning through social and environmental fuel at an unsustainable rate. Put another way, today's conventional management goals, as useful as they may be at producing profitable portfolios, come up short when confronted with broad threats to our social, financial, and environmental systems and indeed often unintentionally contribute to these challenges.[2]

This chapter shows why setting initial goals at a system level is crucial to avoid burning down the house; examines the initial goals conventional, sustainable, and system-level investors set for themselves; and explains the need for formulating goals at a system level.

Conventional Investors' Focus: Maximizing Returns

Elaborated from 1953 through 1972 and put into practice starting in the late 1970s, modern portfolio theory (MPT) was a true revolution in finance. It built on well-established practices that focused on avoiding individually risky securities and put them in the context of sophisticated disciplines for managing risks and rewards at the portfolio level. Fundamental to MPT were a number of axioms, such as the benefits of diversification, the efficiency of markets, and the correspondence of risks taken to rewards received. MPT also assumed that systematic risks—that is, those inherent in the market or in an asset class as a whole— are beyond the ability of asset owners and managers to influence. They therefore should not be penalized or given credit for portfolio losses or gains due to the "systematic" rewards or risks of the market as a whole but only for their own "idiosyncratic" contributions to their portfolios' performance, positive or negative, relative to that of the market.

The long-standing use of MPT speaks to its many advantages. Nevertheless, academics and practitioners in the investment community have recognized that MPT is not without its limitations. Its theoretical constructs assume, for example, that markets operate without transaction costs, have unconstrained liquidity, have a risk-free investment option always available, and are composed of rational actors who consistently act in their own best interest.

Most important, though, is the assumption that the market has risks and rewards that affect investors but that they themselves cannot influence. Whether they are individuals plotting future retirement or institutions addressing future liabilities, the only value that investors can claim for themselves is adding to their portfolios returns that are over those coming from the market as a whole. They only get credit for beating the market— or take the blame if they can't do so.

The global financial crisis of 2008 shook the unquestioning faith in that basic idea. Were not investors' own practices— and their faith in diversification to always protect them from risks—in large part responsible for this global meltdown? Didn't investors' own actions at least in part disrupt the financial system with disastrous consequences? Shouldn't they be held responsible for the damage they were doing? And if so, couldn't investors just as easily inflict the same kind of damage on social and environmental systems and be held responsible for that as well?

At the same time, the financial services industry's size and wealth were growing almost inconceivably. In an increasingly populous and prosperous world of 7.8 billion as of 2020— with rapidly advancing economies in the developing world and increasingly powerful technological tools in ever-increasing availability—estimates of total wealth worldwide in 2019 now run at over $360 trillion.[3]

This substantial size of the financial services industry, both relative to others and in absolute terms, endows its collective actions with an enormous potential for creating unintentional harm. It is only natural that new goals beyond the maximization of portfolio returns by beating the market have emerged as well.

Sustainable Investors' Focus: Social and Environmental Factors

The growing size of the financial markets relative to the overall economy and the diminishing role of governments in regulating those markets have led some investors to intentionally create portfolios with environmental and social benefits. Sustainable investors believe integrating social and environmental considerations into their investments can add value both to society and to their portfolios. When poorly managed, ESG considerations can introduce risks to both; when well managed, they can produce benefits. When these investors consider ESG issues in their decision-making, they might, for example, steer clear of companies that face distracting and costly gender discrimination legal battles, those with frequent sexual harassment lawsuits, or firms that perpetuate dangerous working conditions in developing countries. Alternatively, investors might believe that renewable energy sources (e.g., wind, solar) will replace fossil fuels and invest in them as an attractive long-term investment opportunity.

So, what do sustainable investors care about? There are numerous issues that they might want to address through their investments, and these issues affect industries differently. But they are most likely to encounter certain ones.

The United Nations Sustainable Development Goals (SDGs), for example, provide a useful framework for sustainability issues. Asset managers now frequently reference these goals in marketing and communication materials, in part due to investors' interest and demand. Although some investors and managers have embraced the goals more enthusiastically than others, most will nonetheless acknowledge them.

The seventeen SDGs together target 169 outcomes. These goals can be organized as broad thematic groupings: *people* focuses on ending poverty and hunger and promoting health, equality, and education; *planet* refers to protecting the earth from degradation; *prosperity* aims to ensure that all lives are fulfilling and prosperous; *peace* focuses on "peaceful, just and inclusive societies"; and *partnership* refers to the participation of "all countries, all stakeholders and all people" in achieving the goals.[4]

The Sustainability Accounting Standards Board (SASB) Materiality Map provides a similar framework for determining sustainability issues. An independent organization that sets standards for corporate ESG disclosure, SASB assesses and maps the materiality impact of noteworthy ESG issues across key industry sectors. It does so with an eye to the Securities and Exchange Commission's reporting regulations using a thorough research and vetting process.

SASB has identified thirty issues as reasonably likely to affect the financial condition or operating performance of a company. Its Materiality Map assesses the extent to which relevant issues affect financial performance for ten industry sectors and their key subsectors. These include environmental capital issues like greenhouse gas emissions, energy management, and water and waste management; social and human capital issues like access and affordability, customer welfare, labor relations, and fair labor practices; and governance issues like business ethics and transparency of payments, regulatory capture, and political influence.

System-Level Investors' Focus: Health and Stability of Society, Capital Markets, and the Environment

Conventional investors focus on the efficiency of portfolios to maximize returns that result in long-term utility to society. Sustainable investors focus on generating social and environmental benefit along with financial returns. Both approaches stop short of providing a way for investors to strengthen social, financial, and environmental systems.

In the last fifty years, population growth has increased the labor supply at the same time that a rise in global prosperity and investable assets has increased capital. All this increased growth in labor and capital, along with the economic interconnections they have brought with them, has taken place on a planet with limited resources—that's the one thing that hasn't changed and won't change. The oft-cited remark that "anyone who thinks that you can have infinite growth in a finite environment is either a madman or an economist" rings truer today than ever before.

Investors therefore find themselves in the difficult situation of having to seek the ideal point at which their efficient allocation of assets still functions positively but without harming or otherwise disrupting fundamental systems. Or, in Herman Daly's precise economic language, "The rule is to expand scale (i.e., grow) to the point at which the marginal benefit to human beings of additional man-made physical capital is just equal to the marginal cost to human beings of sacrificed natural capital."[5] The scale of our efficient economy can now cause many of our crucial systems to become fundamentally unstable in ways previously unimaginable.[6]

The Three Sets of Systems Ripe for Instability— and Opportunity

One dramatic example of this instability is the impact of COVID-19. Officially designated a global pandemic by the World Health Organization on March 11, 2020, COVID-19 led to substantial declines in international travel (and domestic travel in some countries), forced closures of schools and "nonessential" businesses, overwhelmed health systems, and brought economic activity in most parts of the world to a near standstill.[7]

COVID-19—and its associated social and economic fallout— shows how social and financial systems (including their underlying business models and supply chains) have become so globalized and interdependent that a disruption to one can wreak havoc on others. Although finance cannot prevent the threat of the next pandemic, intentional system-level decision-making by investors can help prepare for it and mitigate its worst social and economic impacts.

We need better guardrails. By taking a few decisive steps, investors can help put these in place. Investors need to support governments resilient enough and with deep enough pockets to build safeguards and kindle economic recoveries, insist that companies understand their business models and prepare backstops to prevent their meltdown, and prepare for potential systemic breakdowns. With the right tools, investors have the ability to help stabilize these systems while also making long-term, profitable returns.

Three major systems today can benefit from intervention by investors. These systems—social, financial, and environmental—have the potential for high instability, leading to another crash or worse.

Social Systems

Several major corporate trends have created social inequities over the past several decades. They include the maximization of short-term profits at the expense of labor, the tying of CEO compensation to stock price performance, and the movement away from the responsibility for paying a "fair share" of taxes.[8] These shifts have occurred with little regard to their external costs to society or their opportunity costs for the support of basic social and environmental systems, infrastructures, and stakeholders on which sustainable profits and returns ultimately depend.

The relationship between extremes in income inequality and social and political crises is one that investors Ray Dalio, Steven Kryger, Jason Rogers, and Gardner Davis examined in their research on the phenomenon of populism.[9] Key to their findings is that the kind of populism that emerged in the world at the turn of the 20th century and in the 1930s (the periods before and between the two world wars) is analogous to that of today.[10] Extremes like those experienced in those times can lead to conflicts that "typically become progressively more forceful in self-reinforcing ways" and that "often lead to disorder (e.g., strikes and protests)" within countries. They in turn lead to an erosion of democratic governance and the rise of dictatorships.[11] The verdict is still out on how extreme populist sentiments will grow in the coming years, but they are currently manifesting through things like inequality in wealth distribution to a degree rarely seen before; structural unemployment—particularly among the young—that appears to be more than temporary; and winner-take-all industries where a handful of behemoths dominate global markets and take the lion's share of profits.

The importance of inclusive growth is key in the discussions about income inequality and serves to reinforce the wide-ranging agreement about the potentially destabilizing effect the issue has on overarching systems. The International Labor Organization (ILO)—the United Nations agency focused on addressing labor issues globally—has emphasized this dimension in its calls for support for social justice. The growth in inequality, according to the ILO, has not only led to declines in productivity and helped to breed poverty, social instability, and conflict but also led the international community to recognize the need for basic "rules of the game" to ensure globalization promotes equitable prosperity for all.[12]

Some investors are heeding this call and leveraging their assets to promote equal access to a variety of industries for the historically underserved, including digital technology (bridging the digital divide), healthcare (Access to Medicine Index, which reports how twenty pharmaceutical companies make medicines, vaccines, and diagnostics more accessible for people in low- and middle-income countries), financial services (microfinance), and mobile telecommunications.[13]

Still, the siren call of the short term prevents many investors from joining in newer, less conventional endeavors with their long-term benefits to the system as a whole. What investors all must acknowledge is that a long-term view—not bowing to short-term returns over all else—makes it easier to predict and mitigate the nature and extent of the global disruptions to come.

Financial Systems

Scale and short-term profit taking also pose challenges in our financial systems. The lending practices of the early 2000s, with their "robosigning" and packaging of questionable mortgages into diversified fixed-income securities and the willingness of investors around the world to purchase these bonds, were among the root causes of the 2008 financial crisis.[14] In that case, the financial community was placing blind faith in the markets to price securities accurately. In the words of Amar Bhidé, this reliance on the efficiency of financial markets to price is a bit like "driving blindly." As he argues in his book *A Call for Judgment*, "the absolutist prescription to forsake judgment" in assessing financial transactions because one has faith in the efficient pricing of securities has led us

> to blindly trust market prices, [which] not only puts those who follow it at risk, but also undermines the pluralism of opinions that help align prices and values. . . . Forsaking case-by-case judgment . . . is unsustainable en masse: If everyone eschews judgment, who will make market prices even approximately right, or ferret out the offerings of thieves and promoters of worthless securities? Paradoxically, the efficiency of securities markets is a public good that can be destroyed by the unqualified faith of its believers.[15]

Similarly, Stephen Davis, Jon Lukomnik, and David Pitt-Watson, in their book *What They Do with Your Money*, argue that what appear to be innovative financial services creating efficiencies in a complex system have now become at best a drag on the economy and at worst a destabilizing wild card in a system that they believe is "built to fail, at least if success is defined as efficiently promoting our interest."[16]

Since 2008, numerous governmental regulators, industry experts, academics, and public interest groups have proposed stabilizing remedies for this often-abused system. The need for a more active role by government—"adult supervision"—is clear if today's financial system is to better serve the public interest. Evaluating these numerous proposals for government's role is beyond the scope of this book. Many others are tackling that challenge. Rather, we suggest that investors' increasing focus on universal ownership, investment stewardship, long-term value creation, impact investing, ESG integration, and standards setting may play a supporting but essential role to ongoing regulatory measures, lend much-needed stability and a long-term perspective to the financial system, and steer it away from its habits of abuse.

Environmental Systems

When it comes to environmental systems, investors' obsession with short-term efficiency can, and increasingly does, lead to destruction of long-term environmental value.[17] Fossil fuels have long been the most efficient and reasonable energy source. But the scale has now tipped from useful to destructive. Before the 2020 pandemic hit, the global economy burned or otherwise consumed more than 100 million barrels of oil a day, not to mention its use of coal and other fossil fuels.[18] These natural resources have brought tremendous economic benefit without which much of the economic progress since the late 19th century would not have been possible. But this very efficiency is now threatening to destabilize what have been the earth's relatively stable environmental conditions over the past ten thousand years, conditions that have made civilizations as we know them possible.

Tricky challenges like these have been dealt with successfully before. Thirty years ago it became clear that chlorofluorocarbons—Freon and similar gases—were causing damage to the ozone. In 1987, the world adopted the Montreal Protocol, an international agreement designed to protect the ozone layer by phasing out the production of numerous substances that are responsible for ozone depletion. Kofi Annan, the one-time secretary general of the United Nations, referred to the protocol as "perhaps the single most successful international agreement to date."[19] The result is that the ozone hole in Antarctica has slowly recovered, and the ozone layer is expected to return to 1980 benchmark levels in the coming decades.[20]

Scientists point to other looming challenges on environmental fronts. The Stockholm Resilience Centre (SRC), for example, frames these challenges in terms of "planetary boundaries" beyond which unpredictable, catastrophic changes take place. Beyond a certain point, our efficient activities run the risk of fundamentally changing the nature of the earth's environmental systems—nine of them, according to SRC—in ways that we cannot predict but that will cause profound disruptions.[21]

Just as society had to face the unpredictable consequences of the potential destruction of the earth's protective ozone layer from our globally efficient use of Freon, it must now contend with the far more complex task of phasing out fossil fuels to avoid equally problematic uncertainties. But even when the phaseout of fossil fuels is achieved, the underlying problems remain the same: the impacts of scaling up in a populous, interconnected global economy.

These challenges are one of the ways the 21st century will differ from the 20th, and we have to expect and push finance to face these challenges head-on.

Setting System-Level Goals

Three overarching systems, shown in figure 1, require system-level interventions that are highly complex and interconnected. Fortunately, the broad adoption of the Sustainable Development Goals has created an opportunity for investors to think more broadly about their investment goals while also developing concrete investment strategies. Instead of focusing on a simple enumeration of achievements tied to specific investments (e.g., number of affordable housing units created, kilowatts of energy saved, this or that corporate policy changed), they can instead work toward achieving these overall system-level goals.

System-level investors push themselves to achieve goals that focus on the *paradigms* operative at system levels. Paradigms are "philosophical and theoretical frameworks within which we derive theories, laws and generalizations."[22] As a driving force within complex systems, paradigms are a primary contributor to the output of the system. To change the output of a system with a reasonable degree of consistency, one often must change the paradigms that it operates under. The more fundamental a

Social	Financial	Environmental
A series of societal constructs such as equality, well-being, knowledge, theories of law, and other abstract elements that serve as the foundation for society	The laws, contracts, technology, and theoretical and political ideas around which our complicated financial systems have been built	The ecosystems that make up the entirety of our natural world—for example, the oceans, the atmosphere, water, metals, and minerals

Figure 1. Three overarching systems

paradigm shift, the more likely the system is to consistently produce a different output. Using one of the SDGs as an example, investing in the area of *planet* would require a goal of shifting the paradigm of global reliance on fossil fuels.

But a single investor, no matter how large, cannot bring about paradigm shifts alone. Within a complex system, multiple actors and factors are inevitably in play. A causal relationship between a specific investor's input—or any other single factor—and a fundamental paradigm shift is difficult to demonstrate. Influence by multiple parties, however, in bringing about system-level change is a more achievable goal.

For example, in 2017 the Global Investor Coalition on Climate Change, comprising more than 373 investor-members around the world with $35 trillion in assets under management, launched Climate Action 100+, a five-year project committing investors to collaboratively engage more than one hundred of the world's largest greenhouse gas emitters to reduce their carbon emissions. Through this broad-based effort, it is focusing on the largest emitters to increase its chance of shifting practices—and the working paradigm for corporations in general—to substantial reductions of these emissions.[23] Among the members of its steering committee are AustralianSuper, California Public Employees' Retirement System (CalPERS), HSBC Global Asset Management, Ircantec, and Manulife Investment Management.

In its initial 2019 progress report, the coalition noted that its members had already negotiated agreements with major corporations such as AES Corporation (70 percent reduction in carbon intensity by 2030), HeidelbergCement (net zero emissions by 2050), Maersk (net zero emissions by 2050), Nestlé (net zero emissions by 2050), Rio Tinto (exited from coal mining), Volkswagen (climate neutral by 2050), and Xcel Energy (zero carbon electricity by 2050).[24]

The report also sets baseline metrics for measuring future progress. It notes, for example, that companies in most industries have a board member or committee with clear responsibility for climate change—for example, oil and gas (85 percent), industrials (73 percent), and utilities and power producers (74 percent). Relatively few, however, "ensure consistency between their climate-change policy and the positions taken by industry associations of which they are a member"—oil and gas (8 percent), industrials (4 percent), and utilities and power producers (3 percent).[25]

To set goals with relation to paradigm shifts, investors will need to start with an assessment of the current paradigms relating to the system-level challenges with which they are concerned and develop a vision of what alternative paradigms would produce fewer problematic results. With a clear definition of both old and new paradigms in mind, investors can then develop with reasonable specificity goals and milestones for progress.

What Can Investors Do? Think Systemically

This shift toward thinking about the systems in which they invest requires a change in how investors structure their investments. Even those who rely on intermediaries—as most individuals who buy mutual funds or work with financial advisors do—can advance a system-level focus by choosing products and advisors who reflect this awareness.

Investors interested in system-level investing can rely to a certain extent on the techniques developed in the latter half of the 20th century for managing portfolio risks and rewards, but they need a more comprehensive understanding of the effect of these investments on the environment and society. A 2015 report from the Cambridge Institute for Sustainability Leadership, for example, found that "changing asset allocations among various asset classes and regions, combined with investing in sectors exhibiting low climate risk, can offset only half of the negative impacts on financial portfolios brought about by climate change."[26] It's clear that just excluding industries and avoiding bad actors is only half the battle. Investors also need solutions.

By paying attention to the feedback loops between investment practice and social, financial, and environmental systems, system-level investors can set goals that contend with threats that conventional and sustainable investing often ignore. In doing so, these investors acknowledge their impacts on the economy as a whole; their responsibility for stewardship of systems that have been built up over decades, centuries, and eons; and their ability to create long-term value, pursue profit with a purpose, and set social norms. This is a challenge but one that can be overcome by those adopting a new mindset and the right techniques, as we will show in the following chapters.

CHAPTER TWO

Decide Where to Focus

THE PRECEDING chapter outlined the need to set system-level goals. Once goals are in place, the next natural question is, What activities should investors implement? But investors shouldn't rush to this question immediately. Instead, they must first ask a bigger question: *On which issues within which systems should investors focus?*

Deciding where to focus for system-level investors is different from—but nevertheless builds on—how conventional and sustainable investors go about this basic task. Conventional investors are primarily concerned with their selection of managers, styles (active versus passive), asset allocations, and the levels of market risk to be taken. Sustainable investors add the selection of social and environmental challenges they want to tackle as well as the financial instruments appropriate to that task.

System-level investors want to focus in addition on the complex challenges and multiple contributing factors that characterize systems at the highest levels. Relatively simple subsystems may contribute to the larger-scale systems that are these investors' primary concerns, but to get to the heart of the misalignments that cause systems to generate consistently undesirable outcomes, focus at the broadest levels is necessary.

The issue of food security, for example, poses systemic challenges with implications for health, social stability, economic justice, and the environment. Its impacts can cut across all asset classes. The use of chemical pesticides and fertilizers, as environmentally concerning as it may be, is by contrast a subsystem with complex relationships to the broader systems of food security and health. In that sense, it is not a system-level consideration of the broadest sort.[1] Investors might choose to invest in integrated pest management and natural methods of soil enrichment as alternatives, but doing so alone would not address the broadest system-level challenges of food security.

To tackle food security, investors would need to make investments in companies that provide opportunities such as healthy foods, engage with food producers and retailers to reduce sugar in products, and promote outlets that increase access to healthy foods in disadvantaged communities. In addition, system-focused investors might collaborate with their peers or nongovernmental organizations (NGOs) to influence public policy, focusing on issues such as the advertising of unhealthy food to children, the overuse of antibiotics in animal feedstock, and the availability of financial aid to those living with hunger.[2]

One simple measure for distinguishing a system-level issue from others might be this question: Does it impact most or all industries and asset classes? But more detailed criteria are critical for system-level investors to determine the issues on which to focus. The criteria proposed here are consensus as to the issue's importance, its ability to impact investments across all asset classes, the investors' capacity to exercise influence at a system level, and a degree of uncertainty relating to the issue that conventional portfolio risk management techniques cannot address.

Conventional investors focus primarily on the capabilities of their managers to beat investment benchmarks. Sustainable investors add to the mix an intentional focus on creating portfolios with specific and preferably measurable social and environmental benefits. System-level investors focus in addition on identifying the broadest social and environmental challenges for which they can effectively manage risks and rewards.

Counting What Counts as a Systemic Issue

A crucial initial step for investors focusing on system-level issues is to determine which issues are in fact worthy of such consideration. The choice of relevant issues might seem on one level so simple as to not require serious thought. Of course, investors want stable and resilient social, financial, and environmental systems; consequently, any issues involving their preservation or enhancement should be legitimate. In practice, however, choosing a systemic issue can lead to confusion and even abuse.

We propose four criteria here. Essentially, an issue needs to meet all four of these criteria to be relevant for a system-related approach. They are *consensus, relevance, effectiveness*, and *uncertainty*. These criteria can assist long-term investors in assuring that a given system-level issue can be viewed as legitimate and worthy of consideration. These criteria help focus attention on a relatively limited number of issues of overriding relevance with substantial long-term financial implications.[3]

Criterion 1: Consensus

An issue can be judged reasonable for consideration if it has achieved a broad *consensus* as to its legitimacy and general importance, whether positive or negative.[4] The broader that consensus is, the stronger the case for its consideration. Because such issues have achieved consensus as to their legitimacy among a wide range of stakeholders, they can be viewed as a common good, along with the private good of profits or returns. This criterion is intended to ensure that investors consider issues that have been widely debated and do not represent narrowly conceived, idiosyncratic interests.

Wide agreement exists, for example, that a critical function of a well-ordered society is providing for the well-being of its members. Freedom from extreme poverty and the provision of adequate healthcare are typically considered key components of this well-being.[5] The United Nations Human Development Index states that "people and their capabilities should be the ultimate criteria for assessing the development of a country, not economic growth alone."[6] It measures such factors as people's ability to have "a long and healthy life" and have "a decent standard of living."[7] The Organization for Economic Co-operation and Development's Better Life Index rates countries on eleven factors including income and health.[8] The first of the Sustainable Development Goals is to "end poverty in all its forms everywhere" and the third is to "ensure healthy lives and promote well-being for all at all ages."[9] When global consensus-building intergovernmental organizations like the United Nations identify or otherwise call for action on an issue, it helps demonstrate that an issue is systemic in magnitude.

Criterion 2: Relevance

Another criterion is that of relevance. An issue can be judged relevant for consideration if it has substantial potential to impact positively or negatively the long-term financial performance of not simply one portfolio or asset class but portfolios across most industries and asset classes. The greater that potential relevance, the stronger the case for its consideration. When issues impact portfolios across multiple asset classes and industries, investors have no place to hide, and all investors and the general public are impacted.[10]

The criterion of relevance is intended to ensure that investors are considering system-level issues that are broadly pertinent to their long-term financial interests. Matters of the price-related financial performance of specific investments can generally be addressed through risk management at the portfolio level.[11] For issues with broader, longer-term impacts across multiple asset classes—particularly those that result from secular changes, long-tail disruptions, or scientific or geopolitical uncertainties— a system-level view can be helpful.

Income inequality, for example, can profoundly affect investments. In 2014 the Cambridge Centre for Risk Studies published a report on the likely effects of social unrest—which it characterized as a systemic risk of increasing likelihood in the 21st century—on economic development and investment performance. Under three different scenarios of increasing severity, it projected the effects of social unrest on investment performance by asset class and in different geographic regions over a four-year period. For equity portfolios in the United States, it estimated hits of negative 1.76 percent under the least severe of the three scenarios and negative 22.69 percent under the most severe. "What is different and new about the episodes of civil disorder in the early 21st century," the report stated, "is their systemic nature: multiple countries simultaneously expressing dissatisfaction and seeking change." The report singles out youth unemployment among the millennial generation as a likely source of this systemic unrest. Lack of opportunity for many while small segments of the population accumulate great wealth has prompted high-profile concerns about inequality of income and opportunity around the globe.[12]

Similarly, a study by the Sustainability Accounting Standards Boards found climate change to be a "systemic risk"—that is, a material sustainability key performance indicator—for seventy-two of seventy-nine industries that make up the economy.[13]

Criterion 3: Effectiveness

The third criterion relates to the concept of effectiveness. An issue can be considered effective if investors can influence the functioning of a given system, either minimizing potential risks or maximizing rewards.[14] The greater the potential for influence on that system, the stronger the case for consideration. Because risks and rewards are managed at a system level, investors provide a common social good as well as an individual one. This criterion of effectiveness is intended to ensure that long-term investors are considering issues for which their time and resources expended can be effective in producing positive impact upon the systems of relevance to them or in minimizing negative impacts on these systems.

Investors can have a positive impact on health in general and access to healthcare in particular through a variety of policies and practices, for example.[15] They can invest in companies providing health-related products. They can invest in specific companies or technologies that bring down the costs of healthcare. They can invest in those marketing healthcare products and services to individuals and families living in extreme poverty. They can collaborate with governmental, nongovernmental, and corporate organizations working to increase such access.[16] Alternatively, an issue like governmental policies on free and reduced meals in public schools—a public policy of considerable importance—would not be an effective issue for investors to take up because of their limited prospects for influence.

Criterion 4: Uncertainty

The final criterion, uncertainty, relates to whether an issue generates uncertainties that can be positive or negative. The greater the potential for uncertainty due to system-level disruptions, the stronger the case for a system-related approach. When there are uncertainties in the outcomes of complex systems, today's conventional portfolio-risk management tools are not sufficient to meet the challenge; tools designed to act at system levels are required.[17]

This criterion ensures that investors take a system-related approach to reduce the scope of these uncertainties, although they cannot be eliminated entirely. Long-term investors must often contend with what John Maynard Keynes called "the dark forces of time and ignorance which envelop our future."[18] They must understand when their actions might increase the unpredictability and future uncertainty within systems—and to decrease it whenever reasonably possible within the constraints of prudent investment decision-making.

Climate change, for example, involves unpredictability of such broad scope that incorporating it into today's investment policies and practices is a major challenge. Scientists have difficulty predicting something as relatively straightforward as the rate at which sea levels around the world will rise during the 21st century.[19] It is even harder to predict the human migration patterns that will be caused by these increases in sea levels, let alone the social and political impact of that migration. Will major coastal centers of civilization survive? Will nations around the world accept climate-change refugees? It is virtually impossible to predict the answers and equally impossible to incorporate those factors into today's stock valuations. To the degree that investors' decision-making can minimize the likely severity of climate change, it will also minimize the uncertainty that climate change is likely to bring.[20]

Issues that share these four characteristics—consensus, relevance, effectiveness, and uncertainty (table 2)—are those that will be of sufficient concern that long-term investors can reasonably approach them as systemic in nature.

The Criteria in Action: Water

Fresh water provides an example of an issue that is appropriate for system-level investment. This section walks through how an investor considering the global challenges relating to fresh water would determine whether to adopt a system-level approach.

Table 2. Criteria for choosing a system-level issue

| | CRITERIA | | | |
	Consensus	Relevance	Effectiveness	Uncertainty
Definition	An issue that is debated globally and on which agreement about its overriding importance has been achieved.	An issue with substantial potential to impact positively or negatively the long-term financial performance of not simply one portfolio but portfolios across most asset classes.	An issue with substantial potential for investors to influence positively or negatively the functioning of a given system.	An issue with unpredictable and unquantifiable uncertainties if disrupted at a system level.
Importance	Ensures consideration of issues that have been widely debated and that do not represent narrowly conceived, idiosyncratic interests.	Ensures consideration of issues that are broadly relevant, either positively or negatively, to investor's long-term financial interests.	Ensures consideration of issues for which investors' decision-making can be effective in producing positive or negative impact at a system level.	Ensures consideration of issues with substantial potential to create uncertainties and to reduce the scope of these uncertainties.
Examples	The issue of access to fresh water is broadly recognized as a crucial component of societal and environmental systems. Simply put, life is not possible without it.	Positive employee and labor relations are widely seen as crucial to the long-term stability and growth of markets, economies, and firms and hence to investors. High rates of millennial youth unemployment is a current issue of import.	To increase access to healthcare, investors can support companies or technology that reduces costs of products and services (P&S), market P&S to bottom of the pyramid, or collaborate with others to increase such access.	Climate change creates issues with difficult-to-predict outcomes, such as level of sea rise and patterns of forced human migration.

Criterion 1: Consensus

With about one-fifth of the world's population, or 1.2 billion people, living in regions of water scarcity as of 2007, fresh water access is becoming an increasing global challenge.[21] Fresh water plays an essential role in systems supporting life as well as many crucial aspects of our economy. In 2010, the United Nations declared water a human right.[22] In its 2015 annual World Water Development Report, the UN stated that water resources underpin poverty reduction, economic growth, and environmental sustainability. From food and energy security to human and environmental health, water contributes to improvements in social well-being and inclusive growth, affecting the livelihoods of billions.[23] Because of the broad recognition of water as a systemic challenge, it meets the requirements of the consensus criterion.

Criterion 2: Relevance

Numerous studies have documented the importance of the availability of high-quality fresh water to economic development and hence to long-term investment opportunity.[24] Water capacity constraints can limit the growth of industry. The pollution of rivers and groundwater can cause health problems and impact food and beverage production. Drought can devastate economies and kill through famine when crops wither and die. Workforce productivity can be lost to illness from contaminated drinking water and to the demands on domestic time in obtaining water in many regions. Fresh water, in its multiplicity of uses, is relevant to investment across industries and asset classes.[25]

Criterion 3: Effectiveness

Investment opportunities abound for increasing the availability of water, improving its efficiency, and assuring its quality. These include water infrastructure systems, wastewater treatment systems, pollution control devices, water usage metering, irrigation equipment, desalination technologies, and filtration and pumping products, among many others. In addition, opportunities for investors to work collaboratively to effect positive change, such as the Ceres Investor Water Hub, are taking shape. Therefore, investors can have an effective impact on this issue.[26]

Criterion 4: Uncertainty

The long-term social and economic consequences of the fact that glaciers worldwide are in retreat and an estimated one-third of aquifers worldwide are being overdrawn create global environmental and social uncertainties with profound social and investment implications that are likely to persist for decades to come.[27] Specifically, if access to water accounted for by glaciers and aquifers is lost, it will be virtually impossible to predict the consequences with any degree of certainty.[28] An estimated 2 billion people living in a dozen Asian countries depend on rivers such as the Ganges, Indus, Yangtze, and Mekong, which are fed in large part by the dependable runoff from thousands of glaciers in the high Tibetan plateau.[29] California's fruitful farms depend on the reliability of the Sierra Nevada snowpack for much of their summer water supply.[30] Midwestern farmers draw on the vast aquifers of that region.[31] Addressing climate change and supporting the preservation of fresh water systems would therefore reduce uncertainty in the market.

Taking the First Steps

Only a limited number of issues rise to the level at which applying a system-level approach is appropriate. They include those that have achieved widespread consensus as to their systemic importance, are broadly relevant to long-term investment returns, are susceptible to substantive influence from investors, and have a broad range of uncertain implications and a limited number of outcomes.[32] In addition to climate change and income inequality, other system-level issues include environmental themes such as biodiversity, oceans, access to fresh water, natural resources, and sustainable land use; social themes such as consumer health and safety, human rights, social equity and diversity, and pandemics; and financial themes such as shareholder rights, market transparency, and financial market stability.

Once investors—institutions or individuals—have committed themselves to a system-level approach and focused on a 21st century challenge with broad systemic implications, they must then confront the question of what actions they can effectively take. The answer to this question is addressed in the next three chapters. First, they can allocate their investments to asset classes well suited to address the particular challenge of concern (chapter 3). Second, they can extend traditional investment practice so that it intentionally contends with systemic risks and rewards in addition to those at portfolio levels (chapter 4). Third, they can adopt new techniques that are explicitly designed to influence systems themselves and that can help prevent undesirable outcomes from occurring in the first place, rather than struggling with them once they occur (chapter 5).

CHAPTER THREE

Allocate Assets

THE F. B. Heron Foundation, a private foundation focused on community economic development, describes itself as operating "at the intersection of community and capital markets" and seeks to use its investments as tools along with its grants to empower people and institutions in low-income communities. In 2019, to address the disjunction between the rich agricultural corporations operating in the San Joaquin Valley of California and the poor conditions of many workers there, it chose two fixed-income investments—loans and bonds—to support Self-Help Enterprises (SHE), a local nonprofit it viewed as equipped to play a key role in bettering the overall lives of these farmworkers. Fixed-income investments, especially when issued by the government and to support nonprofits, are particularly well suited to build baseline infrastructure and public goods that can produce positive outcomes.[1]

Heron initially made a $1 million ten-year below-market-rate loan (a "program-related investment") to the organization to establish a long-term base for SHE's operations. Soon after, it identified a market-rate bond issued by the California Health Facilities

Financing Authority that funded two of SHE's projects along with similar initiatives in the region. So it added a $1 million slice of this issuance to its endowment's market-rate portfolio.[2]

As far back as its founding in 1992, Heron had contended with the challenge of how to use its grant-making most effectively to achieve its community development goals. It first departed from conventional philanthropic norms by focusing on grants to support operating budgets rather than programmatic themes. Heron also began making what it calls "enterprise capital grants," which channel substantial up-front funds to grantees for quantum organizational leaps, much as venture capital does in the for-profit world.

In 2005, it began considering how to use all the "tools in its toolbox" to better support this mission. A key component in this strategy became aligning the investment of its endowment's assets with its grant-making. Between 2012 and 2016 it transitioned 100 percent of its endowment's holdings to achieve community-focused outcomes. To make this shift in its equity investments, Heron developed its customized US Community Investing Index (USCII). The USCII sets a model for publicly traded companies for community-oriented management of four sources of stakeholder "capital": human (employees and suppliers), civic (government, customers, and neighbors), natural (environmental inputs and outputs), and financial (boards and investors, and management).[3]

Using Asset Classes for System-Level Change

As seen in the Heron Foundation example, investors large and small can think creatively about how to use asset classes for social and environmental impact. The first step is always to decide what asset classes to use: stocks or bonds, venture capital or real estate, private equity or cash. Of course, investors want their money back with a return. Some asset classes historically have returned more than others, some are quite risky, and each serves different societal functions.

Conventional investors typically balance their desired returns with their tolerance for risk, and their need for income with their prospects for market appreciation. They don't factor social and environmental risks and opportunities into the equation.

Sustainable investors, once having decided on their asset allocation, select individual securities within it that are aligned with their social and environmental goals.

System-level investors take one further step. They consider how to use each asset class to maximize the societal benefits it was originally designed to create. Fixed income, for example, can naturally create public goods when issued by governments. Public equities are well suited to influence incremental change in large firms. Venture capital is a disruptor of business models and services.

Two broad asset classes dominate the investment landscape: equities (ownership) and debt (lending). Each has variations. Ownership can take the form of public equities, private equity, and venture capital and can also include real estate and infra-structure. Lending consists of bonds, direct loans, and to a certain extent cash. System-level investors understand that each asset class provides specific societal benefits and that they can partici-pate in these asset classes in ways that enhance their benefits.

Equities

Equities include public equities, private equity, and venture capital.

PUBLIC EQUITIES

Public equities are stocks in large corporations that facilitate the trading of ownership positions by institutions and individuals. Public equities are traded on public exchanges. The market for public equities was created in part so that investors large and small could share in these large corporations' profits and so that these corporations in turn could raise funds from the full range of potential investors. Hence a first benefit: companies enjoying the efficiencies of their large scale can more easily raise capital and at the same time broadly share their profits. But since the public is involved, the government requires these companies to disclose their financials and business strategies. Hence a second benefit: investors now have data and access to pressure these corporations to operate efficiently and presumably in their and the public's long-term interests.

Today's conventional investors typically just want to buy stocks that will go up or pay a handsome dividend. They don't see a particular benefit in considering corporations' social and environmental behavior. In fact, they believe those considerations can often interfere with a company's ability to maximize its returns.

Sustainable investors, on the other hand, intentionally add to their portfolios companies aligned with their own social and environmental goals and encourage managers of these firms to improve practices that can enhance their social benefits along with their profitability.

System-level investors use their public equity investments to set models for corporate behavior across all industries for key stakeholders and for industries' overall management of issues that at a system level pose risks or offer rewards.

The California State Teachers' Retirement System (CalSTRS) provides one example of what leveraging public equities at a system level looks like in practice. It has determined that climate change is a systemic risk and developed a multiyear, multi-asset-class, internally managed Low-Carbon Index (LCI) for passive equity management. Launched in 2017 with a $2.5 billion commitment, the LCI is made up of stocks in all industries in all markets (US, developed, and emerging) around the world. CalSTRS's goal is for these holdings to have reduced carbon emissions and reserves in each market by between 61 percent and 93 percent in the coming years.[4] Since passive index funds hold hundreds, if not thousands, of stocks across all industries, the CalSTRS index will paint a picture of what the future should look like in all companies around the world, in effect setting a benchmark and model for the environmental performance of large corporations on climate change.

Moreover, through its stewardship program, CalSTRS joins with its peers to urge emissions reductions by the most systematically important firms worldwide. It led, for example, the Climate Action 100+ collaborative engagement with Duke Energy in 2019, which negotiated that company's commitment to reduce carbon dioxide (CO_2) emissions by more than 50 percent by 2030 and achieve net-zero CO_2 emissions by 2050. CalSTRS has also pressured oil and gas companies to cut their methane emissions, having filed ten shareholder resolutions urging action since

2015, half of which led to negotiated settlements.[5] In addition, as part of its efforts to shift the balance of its active managers of stocks in this same direction, in 2019 it hired three new firms with proven expertise in sustainability issues.[6] Although it uses divestment only as a last resort, in 2017 it ceased investments in companies deriving more than 50 percent of revenues from sale of thermal coal.[7]

CalSTRS is not the only large investor to use a low-carbon index to drive home the point about where large corporations should be headed. In 2019, the New York State Common Retirement Fund released a Climate Action Plan aimed at providing a road map "to address climate risks and opportunities across all asset classes."[8] It has established a $20 billion goal for its Sustainable Investment and Climate Solutions Program. A key component of this initiative is a $4 billion commitment to a broad-market passively managed equities index of low-emissions firms. This index fund is internally managed, and companies with poor performance are prioritized for engagement. In 2018 the fund pressured ten firms to set emissions reductions goals in line with the Paris Agreement.[9]

Establishing their own customized indexes of large, publicly traded companies as CalSTRS has done for climate change and Heron Foundation has done for community economic development is just one way that investors can look to move large corporations as a whole toward systemic change.

PRIVATE EQUITY

Private equity consists of direct ownership by investors—individuals or institutions—in for-profit enterprises. Owners, few in number, benefit from the freedom to run a firm as they will. They can reinvest profits in their firms or take them for themselves. They need not disclose their finances, business strategies, or management practices to the public.

Conventional investors typically allocate assets to large private equity funds that in turn buy and sell private firms and share the profits from these transactions with their investors. Alignment with social and environmental goals is not part of the picture.

Sustainable investors set out to find and use private equity fund managers that do incorporate such social and environmental concerns and impose them on the management of the companies they buy and sell. The portfolios of these funds may make investments that address aspects of poverty alleviation, renewable energy, food security, or other social and environmental challenges.

Among the steps that system-level investors take to enhance their impact and set new models for this asset class is to cut out the middleman—that is, the equity funds. Doing so gives investors in private equity full knowledge of and control over their investments' business models and practices, as well as their social and environmental impacts. Not incidentally, direct investment also spares them the sometimes substantial fees that intermediary fund managers charge. These advantages represent a systemically important enhancement of today's private equity investment model.

For instance, the Caisse de dépôt et placement du Québec (CDPQ), one of Canada's largest pension funds, makes substantial use of direct private equity in a hands-on approach to promoting economic growth and resilience at a local level in the cities and regions in which its beneficiaries live.[10] Among other investments, it has made a major multiyear commitment to private equity investment in the infrastructure of Montreal to boost the city's appeal as a commercial and tourist destination. CDPQ is the primary investor in and general contractor for the construction of a rapid-transit extension of the city's subway system that will connect downtown Montreal with the city's airport. Simultaneously, it has made major commitments to the revitalization of the city's downtown real estate, including investments in malls, hotels, and restaurants. It has also created a $250 million private equity fund earmarked for artificial intelligence businesses in Canada—with $170 million initially invested in three companies: Element AI, Dialogue, and Talent .com.[11] It has diversified its direct private equity holdings globally, stressing many of the same social and environmental themes. In Australia, for example, it has invested $150 million in a 24.9 percent stake in a partnership involved in the Sydney Metro mass-transit system.[12]

Institutional investors have the assets and in-house expertise to take advantage of direct private equity. Wealthy individuals may invest in private equity funds aligned with their sustainability goals or make direct investment primarily through family offices if they have personal knowledge of specific industries. Individuals can urge their pension funds or the endowments of the nonprofits to which they contribute to take a sustainable or systemic approach to this asset class.

VENTURE CAPITAL

Venture capital is an asset class designed for rapid disruptive change. In the hands of system-level investors, this approach to equity ownership, along with investments in some small-scale private equity and small-capitalization publicly traded stocks, can aim at creating business models that solve the most challenging systemic risks or create corresponding rewards.

Sustainable investors might remain content with simple alignment with a theme, such as one of the SDGs, but not seek venture capital investments that go to the heart of solving a systemic challenge. For example, to achieve alignment with the SDG of ensuring healthy lives, they might invest in early-stage firms with innovative solutions to treating a disease but without addressing the underlying nature of the disease's causes. And conventional investors may not care whether an innovative, disruptive business model, although profitable, has systemic impacts as harmful as they are beneficial—for example, firms with business models relying on a precarious gig-economy workforce.

In practice, investors in systemically focused "solutions" funds can be large as well as small. Institutional investors, for example, have solutions-oriented funds targeted to renewables. As of 2019, CalSTRS, mentioned above with regard to its approach to public equities, had invested $691 million in a private equity clean energy portfolio and $505 million in "solar, wind, and other renewable power and LEED [Leadership in Energy and Environmental Design] certified assets."[13] In addition, numerous small and midsized investment managers offer renewable energy funds open to individual investors and investing in publicly traded companies.

Fixed Income and Loans

Bonds, along with direct lending, form the second large class of investments. Bonds and loans start with a simple purpose and from there branch out into an almost infinitely varied, flexible, and customizable world of products and services. Among their societal benefits is providing organizations and individuals with access to substantial chunks of up-front cash for expenditures that they can't immediately come up with but can pay back over time. Both bonds and loans are of immense value in promoting economic activity, although the specific purposes to which borrowed funds are put may or may not benefit society.

BONDS

Bonds are securities that facilitate the trading of loans by institutions and individuals. These may be large loans to governments and corporations for general or specific purposes. Or they may be bundles of small loans made to real estate purchasers (e.g., mortgages) or consumers (e.g., credit card debt). These bonds promise a regular flow of payments to their investors (the "coupon") and have evolved into a huge, diverse, and complicated asset class.

When issued by national or local governments or by nonprofit organizations, bonds are attractive to system-level investors because they can fund public goods such as affordable housing and small business development. They can also support basic physical and intangible societal infrastructures—such as those essential to transportation, water treatment, education, and healthcare—that build a long-term foundation for economic stability and hence for investment opportunities.

Conventional investors typically allocate assets to bonds based on their expectations for risk-adjusted returns, not their ability to support the government or create public goods. Sustainable investors, once they have decided on their allocation to fixed income, will often align the types and specifics of the fixed-income securities they select for their portfolios with their own social or environmental goals—for example, the UN Sustainable Development Goals.

System-level investors go a step further, participating in the creation of and standards setting for what are essentially markets for new types of bonds. The development of the green bond market illustrates this point. Starting in 2007, a handful of development financial institutions began issuing what they described as "green bonds" that funded projects such as renewable energy, water, and green buildings and transportation. What exactly qualified as "green," however, was not clear. As investors' demand for these bonds grew, the need for standardized principles for what in fact constituted "green" became apparent. This gap in the market led to the development of several sets of voluntary "principles" for green bonds devised by the financial industry and other stakeholders.

These principles were key to the market's continued growth: approximately \$250 billion in new green bonds were issued in 2019, bringing the total investments in this new market to close to \$1 trillion.[14] Bank of America (BoA) is an example of a financial services firm that participated systematically in this market's development. From the outset, BoA played a prominent role as a lead underwriter of green bonds. Through 2019 it had also issued six green bonds of its own, funding \$6.35 billion in clean energy initiatives.[15] In addition, it participated in the creation of the International Capital Market Association's voluntary Green Bond Principles and continues to sit on its executive committee.

Some investors, seeing the need for a governmental role to bring further systemization to the market, have supported the European Union's current development of a universal taxonomy for green bonds, which will constitute a further step in the regularization and legitimization of this market. The Scandinavian financial services firm Nordea Group is one of the seven members of the Green Bond Standards Working Group, which is providing technical advice to the EU as it intervenes at this key leverage point within the complex fixed-income world of investments.

The success of green bonds has also prompted the emergence of a related market for "social" bonds and, when the pandemic hit, for "COVID" bonds in particular. In the first five months of 2020, $151.5 billion was raised globally through issuance of COVID bonds.[16] This proliferation of socially and environmentally targeted bonds illustrates how demand from investors and participation in standards setting can bring about key changes in the fixed-income market.

SOVEREIGN DEBT

The ratings for sovereign debt—bonds issued by national governments around the world—are another area where investors are leaving their mark.

For conventional investors in sovereign debt, geopolitical and governance risk factors have long figured among their considerations. Sustainable investors in increasing numbers are integrating an additional set of environmental, social, and governance concerns. At the security selection and portfolio construction levels, ESG factors are now finding their way into the analyses of these sustainability investors, although as one 2019 report noted, "Few investors integrate ESG factors *systematically* into their sovereign debt portfolios" (italics in the original).[17]

Investors with an eye on systemic risk see ESG integration into portfolio construction, where pricing of risk is a primary concern, as a stepping-stone to a more holistic approach. For instance, the Swiss investment management firm RobecoSAM now incorporates evaluation of systemic risk factors in its Country Sustainability Ranking. Several of these risk factors touch on complex, difficult-to-value indicators such as governments' natural capital management (e.g., ecosystem vitality, environmental status), human capital (e.g., gender inequality, confidence in government), and management of political rights (e.g., management of public goods, civil liberties).[18]

These systemic risk factors are not easily translatable into price. Their benefit to investors, though, is that they can become a lever for pressuring governments to address systemic risks and rewards. One starting point for applying such pressure is the creation of investable indexes based in part on these systemic factors. Along those lines, RobecoSAM's Country Sustainability ranking, which includes these systemic indicators, is the basis for the S&P ESG Sovereign Bond Index Family.[19]

LOANS

Typically, institutional investors make limited use of direct loans as an asset class. They are, however, becoming increasingly vocal on the social and environmental risks implicit in how commercial and retail banks set about their lending.

Historically, major banks have been essentially agnostic as to the social and environmental impacts of their loans. That has started to change as investors with a sustainable and system-level perspective express ever greater concern. Banks are of course prohibited from doing business with criminal elements. But more and more they are being told to limit or are voluntarily limiting their financing for activities that can be viewed as posing systemic risks. Here are a few examples:

- Eight European countries have laws on their books that prohibit investments in production of cluster bombs, antipersonnel weapons, and similar armaments. Three of these—Belgium, Spain, and Switzerland—also prohibit their financing.[20]

- As of 2016, six large US financial services firms—Bank of America, Citigroup, Goldman Sachs, JPMorgan Chase, Morgan Stanley, and Wells Fargo—limited to some extent their financing of coal mining firms.[21]

- In 2017, the Dutch bank ABN AMRO announced that it would make no new loans to tobacco companies.[22]

More generally, in 2019 in conjunction with the United Nations Environment Programme Finance Initiative, 132 banks launched the Principles for Responsible Banking, which committed signatories to "continuously increase our positive impacts while reducing the negative impacts on, and managing the risks to, people and environment resulting from our activities, products and services." Whether this first voluntary step toward a more systematic, firm-level approach to the implications of their lending will have practical impact remains to be seen, but at a minimum it represents a symbolic shift in these financial institutions' public stance.[23]

A NOTE ON CASH

Cash, though used only marginally as an asset class by institutional investors, is well suited to support local community development. Institutional investors tend to use cash only as a short-term, low-risk, low-reward place to park funds while waiting for attractive opportunities elsewhere to develop.

For individuals, by contrast, savings and checking accounts are often an important part of their assets. By placing these funds with banks or credit unions that are strong supporters of local communities and businesses, they can support sustainability goals. Certain credit unions, such as the North Carolina–based Self-Help Credit Union and the Mississippi-based Hope Credit Union, and privately held banks, such as the California-based Beneficial State Bank and the Arkansas-based Southern Bancorp, provide models for confronting systemic challenges such as poverty and discrimination.

Real Assets

Among other things, real assets consist of residential and commercial real estate and of infrastructure such as bridges, roads, ports, airports, mass transit, and the like.

REAL ESTATE

Real estate is an unusual asset class. For individuals, ownership of a home is often their primary investment, dramatically more so than other asset classes. As an asset, it is unique in that they live in and attend to it every day. In that sense their real estate investment can become the physical embodiment of their personality. Those committed to sustainability principles can, for example, directly invest in environmental commitments such as the use of renewable energy within that physical asset that surrounds them. By contrast, direct ownership of residential property is an investment to which institutional investors typically do not allocate substantial assets and, when they do so, can become controversial in that they are absentee landlords.

Commercial and industrial real estate is also a part of the built environment, and its environmental impacts therefore also become part of the responsibility of its owners. Sustainable investors—institutions or individuals—participating in this aspect of real estate have several options. Some are indirect: they can factor large corporations' management of their properties into their equities investment policies, or they can invest in publicly traded real estate investment trusts that take the social and environmental concerns of their holdings into account (e.g., Vert Asset Management). They can also invest in the projects of real estate developers that focus on transit-oriented projects, employ union labor, or adopt other social and environmental practices. CalPERS, for example, is among those public pension funds with a "responsible contractor policy" with regard to the labor practices for those holdings in its real estate portfolio.

Individuals might be considered to be taking a system-level approach to their investment in home ownership if they were advocates for green energy or affordable housing throughout their neighborhood or region. Similarly, institutional investors can take a systemic risk management approach by promoting the adoption and implementation of environmental and social standards throughout the commercial real estate asset class.

INFRASTRUCTURE

Infrastructure is also part of the built environment and as such has profound social and environmental impacts. System-level investors can look beyond the financial or social returns of particular opportunities to the use of multiple, coordinated infrastructure investments to catalyze economic development and empowerment throughout a particular locality. For example, a city's or region's transportation systems can play a key role in economic prospects and similarly its environmental footprint.

Prudential Financial, which appears again at the beginning of chapter 4 as an example of how an investor can extend conventional and sustainable investment practices to encompass a systemic approach, has used a coordinated set of infrastructure and impact investments in a concentrated set of interconnected initiatives to help revitalize downtown Newark, New Jersey. As part of this $1.1 billion initiative, Prudential has made $500 million in infrastructure investments and $438 million in impact investments, which it has supplemented with $197 million in grants and corporate contributions.[24]

Among its infrastructure projects in Newark are the headquarters for its Prudential Global Investment Management division; a nearly $50 million investment in the renovation of the former Hahne department store into a multiuse building including 160 units of affordable and market-rate housing, an arts and cultural incubator, a food supermarket, restaurants, and retail stores;[25] and a $6 million investment in the West Ward's Georgia King Village 422-unit affordable housing complex. In addition, among its support for local business is a $5.25 million investment in AeroFarms, an innovative indoor farming company headquartered in Newark. Prudential supplements these investments with grants to build out the public and nonprofit infrastructure of downtown. For example, it contributed $2 million to the renovation of Military Park in downtown and has made $29 million in donations to the New Jersey Performing Arts Center, also in Newark.[26]

Target Asset Classes to Leverage Points

Whether investors are foundations, pension funds, family offices, or individuals, the positive potential social and environmental impacts of the asset classes in which they choose to invest—and how those social and environmental impacts for which they are well suited can be enhanced—are important considerations. The more that investors can target their use of asset classes as a whole to key leverage points that allow systems to generate positive outcomes from the start, the greater their contribution will be to a rising tide of investment opportunities for themselves and for other investors—and the more closely they can align their policies and practices with long-term systemic goals.

CHAPTER FOUR

Apply Investment Tools

DURING THE "Long Hot Summer of 1967," nearly 160 race riots erupted across the United States over the course of several months. Racial tensions spurred on by years of discrimination, unemployment, and substandard living conditions finally boiled over in the form of rioting, looting, and property destruction. The impact on Newark, New Jersey, was particularly hard: twenty-six people died, hundreds more were injured, and the city was devastated for decades.[1]

Newark has recovered substantially from that challenging moment in its history. Since the 1960s, the city has cycled through upswings and downturns, but Prudential Financial, the global financial services behemoth, has since its founding in 1875 maintained its headquarters there. Prudential is widely considered one of the anchor institutions of the city and has supported Newark's economic revitalization since the 1970s through its financial inclusion initiatives and support for underserved neighborhoods. Between 1976 and 2016, it invested $2.6 billion to impact investment projects around the world, $1 billion of that to economic revitalization of Newark through both its impact investment programs and philanthropic activities.[2]

One of its subsidiaries, Prudential Global Investment Management (PGIM), operates an impact investment fund through its Prudential Impact Investments (PII) unit. This fund is an example of how an investor can extend the use of conventional investment techniques to address a systemic issue: the challenges of local poverty alleviation, affordable housing, youth training, access to capital, and income inequality.[3]

If PGIM were a purely conventional investor, its decision-making might have remained narrowly focused on security valuation and portfolio diversification, ignoring social and environmental considerations and the city around it. If it had brought in considerations related to sustainable investing, it might have offered a fund that integrated ESG considerations, avoiding investments with poor ESG performance and including those with positive impact while earning competitive financial returns. It might have offered a global fund that excluded companies that produced weapons or that generated a percentage of their revenue from the manufacture of tobacco products, or it might not have invested in government bonds from countries with a record of human rights violations (e.g., Burma or Sudan). Or it might have emphasized investments in companies that had positive ESG practices or specific environmental or social benefits. Or PGIM could have engaged with companies in its portfolios to improve their ESG policies and practices and reduce ESG risks through direct communication (e.g., writing letters or meeting with companies), exercising shareholder voting rights (directly or through a third party), and filing shareholder resolutions. It might have urged a company to address risks posed by poor labor relations in its production and supply chains, resource scarcity, new environmental regulations, or inadequate commitments to diversity.

Instead, PII made $1 billion in community-focused impact investments between 2014 and 2020. PII is a solutions-oriented fund that strives to advance economic and social mobility for underserved populations. It invests in both for-profit and non-profit enterprises, with a focus on those promoting financial inclusion by investing in microfinance organizations, community development financial institutions in the United States, and financial services companies in the developing world, as well as organizations promoting job training and skills development in underserved communities.[4]

Through its investments targeted at infrastructure and economic development impact in Newark, along with grant giving targeted to these same two purposes, Prudential has learned from its long-term investment in Newark that once an investor chooses a specific issue to dedicate itself to, it can systematically target investments toward specific social and environmental solutions through a program of interrelated and interconnected investments. (See chapter 3 for details on this locally targeted initiative.)

Investors like PGIM extend a variety of conventional and sustainable investment practices to put system-level strategies into effect. Some extend familiar practices such as security selection and portfolio construction to attain specific systemic goals. Others use their statements of investment beliefs, engagement programs, or manager selection to incorporate system-level perspectives.[5]

The fundamentals of these activities are not new to investors. Most are already well established as part of mainstream portfolio management. But their use has been expanded to incorporate systemic perspectives.

The difference between the conventional implementation of these activities and their use in system-level investing is that system-level investing not only incorporates these key investment activities into the management of risks and rewards at the portfolio level but also sees how they can be applied within a system-level context. This chapter provides examples of investors that are making this transition with regard to investment beliefs, security selection and portfolio construction, engagement, and manager selection.

Including System-Level Concerns in Investment Beliefs

Investors often state their beliefs—their guiding assertions— about how financial markets work and how their activities relate to those markets. Along with their investment policy statement, investors may have a formal investment beliefs statement (IBS), although this is not the only form in which their beliefs may appear. An IBS articulates the fundamental perceptions of investors on the nature of financial markets and the role they play in them. An IBS is important because it helps trustees and others clarify their views, sets forth an institution's rationale for its selection of investment styles and managers, and guides its strategic decisions and goals.[6]

Conventional investors might assert their belief that the financial markets are efficient or that they leave room for active managers to exploit inefficiencies or that taking greater risks is rewarded with higher returns. Sustainable investors might express the belief that proactive consideration of ESG issues will reduce risk and generate long-term value. They may state that they have a responsibility to generate positive social impact alongside their pursuit of financial return and that positive social and financial returns are not mutually exclusive.[7]

Investors with a system-level focus extend their beliefs to the social, financial, and environmental systems that pose threats to or offer opportunities for their investments across all asset classes. They might go further still and assert that the synergistic relationship between these three systems means that a threat to the health of one impacts the health of the others.[8]

CalPERS—which is discussed again in chapter 5—is an example of how a beliefs statement can take a systemic perspective. CalPERS states that it "believes that encouraging our external managers, portfolio companies, and policy makers to engage in responsible environmental practices is important to risk management. This means making wise use of scarce resources, considering impact, and addressing *systemic risks*, such as climate change" (emphasis added).[9]

Another example is that of Mercer, a subsidiary of Marsh & McLennan Companies, a financial consultant firm and asset owner. It states that "at Mercer, we believe an investment approach that includes environmental, social and corporate governance (ESG) factors and broader *systemic issues*—for example, climate change and sustainable development—along with active ownership (stewardship) is more likely to lead to sustainable investment outcomes, such as a greater ability to sustain pension payments" (emphasis added).[10]

The Washington State Investment Board (WSIB), a public pension fund, explains in its formal investment beliefs statement that as a long-term investor it "is subject to complex and *systemic global risks* that unfold over time, including financial risks resulting from global climate change" (emphasis added). Despite some of these risks being "difficult to quantify," WSIB considers "all identifiable risks in [its] investment process and believe[s] thoughtful consideration of these evolving global challenges is inseparable from long-term investment strategy and performance."[11]

These beliefs statements can be short or long, detailed or general, comprehensive or selective. Whatever the form, they address those issues that are the important drivers of an investor's investment process, that are core to its investment practices, and that distinguish it clearly from others.[12] The challenge, which can be substantial for investors, is to identify those beliefs that are credible and appropriate to the institution itself and likely to remain so for the indefinite future. (To support the identification of those beliefs, investors can use the criteria for choosing a system-level issue detailed in chapter 2.)

Emphasizing System Fortifiers in Security Selection and Portfolio Construction

Security selection and portfolio construction are the incorporation of risk-control and related considerations into the investment process. For sustainable investors and increasingly conventional investors these days, these include the integration of ESG factors into security selection when financially material. This helps sustainable investors proactively identify companies with relatively strong ESG performance or avoid those with poor performance; they can also integrate these considerations into ongoing monitoring.[13] For conventional investors it adds another factor to their risk models. For both, it stops at the management of risks and opportunities at a portfolio level.

Investors with system-related concerns may extend this process to the setting of standards or minimum thresholds for social and environmental conduct for whole industries based on problematic business models (say, fossil fuels) or issues (say, human rights).[14] Concerns about the systemic risks of climate change have recently prompted such investors to progress from concerns about its risks for one particular company or another to setting standards for involvement in the coal or oil and natural gas industries in general. Chapter 8 includes a description of the Rockefeller Brothers Fund's journey along this road. It is far from the only investor to have recently extended its use of divestment from single fossil-fuel firms to the industry more generally.[15]

The converse of divestment and exclusion is investment and inclusion. Impact investors identify individual examples of opportunities to create social and environmental benefits in areas as diverse as healthcare, the environment, fair labor, and diversity. A few have extended this practice to create concentrated investment programs aimed at systematic change in one issue or region.

In Quebec, with its increasing need for sustainable and inclusive economic growth, the pension fund Caisse de dépôt et placement du Québec, introduced in chapter 3, is an example of an investor that has stepped in to fill this gap. CDPQ is a highly rated pension plan with over $340 billion in assets under management, including $3.3 billion in private investments and commitments to the Quebec private sector in 2019.[16] To fulfill its legislatively mandated mission of promoting the economic development of the province, CDPQ has adopted a threefold approach. First, it emphasizes growth and globalization to finance and support Quebec companies of all sizes. Next, CDPQ focuses on innovation and the next generation, contributing to developing new-economy ecosystems and supporting innovative companies, in addition to stimulating entrepreneurship. Lastly, CDPQ invests in impact projects; designing, developing, and financing major infrastructure and real estate projects; and supporting the renewable energy sector.

CDPQ has adopted and implemented a sustainability program for much of the real estate property that it owns and manages through its Ivanhoé Cambridge and Otéra Capital subsidiaries. Ivanhoé Cambridge, among the largest global asset managers, has approximately $49 billion in assets. Many of its real estate investments support infrastructure and business development in Quebec. Most of its real estate investments have environmental certification, and many contribute to the revitalization of Montreal's downtown. Not only did these investments grow the pension plan of the Quebec groups that bought into the plan, but they helped bolster the economy where their beneficiaries live.[17]

Engaging Corporations on Systemic Considerations

Conventional investors have long had ways to communicate with corporate managers when dissatisfied with a company's financial performance. The "Wall Street Walk" is simply selling their stocks. These days "activist" hedge fund and private equity investors pressure companies to break up their operations, fire management, and take other dramatic steps to improve returns to stockowners.

Sustainable investors frequently engage individual companies to improve their environmental, social, and governance policies and practices and reduce ESG risks. They do so through direct communication (e.g., writing letters or meeting with companies), exercising shareholder voting rights (directly or through a third party), and filing shareholder resolutions.[18] At the low end of the spectrum, investors write letters to a company, vote their proxies, conduct in-person meetings, sign on to letters with other shareholders, meet with the CEO or board, file a shareholder resolution, and build support for such resolutions. On the high end, they engage in "vote no" campaigns against directors or key committees, run a candidate for the board, and, in the most extreme cases, file lawsuits.[19] They do so to improve both the company's financial performance and its social or environmental performance.

System-level investors can extend engagement beyond activism or engagement with individual firms by joining in efforts to change systems at the core. The progress of one engagement by the Swedish national AP pension funds' Council on Ethics shows how this approach can produce results.

The council is an organization set up as a collaborative effort of four of these AP funds. Its mandate is to influence companies through active dialogue. In 2015 it began an engagement with the mining company Vale when a tailing pond at one of the firm's Brazilian operations burst. Four years later, a second tailing pond dam in Brazil collapsed, killing over 250 people.

At that point the council recommended that the AP funds divest their Vale holding—but it didn't stop there. It joined a coalition of other investors spearheaded by the Church of England Pensions Board to address the source of the problem throughout the mining industry. That effort led to demands for a global standard for best practice in the management of tailing operations and the creation of a database for the public sharing of information on eighteen hundred tailing dams operated by mining, oil, and gas companies worldwide.[20] (See chapter 8 for further details on the Church of England Pensions Board's role.) In the council's words, in 2007 it "started its company engage-ments with individual companies, then with experience based on those expanded to sector wide pro-active engagements and we are now engaging the problem."[21]

To address the long-term risks to investments posed by poor labor relations in production and supply chains, natural resource scarcity, new environmental regulations, or gender diversity, among other issues posing systemic challenges, investors can elevate their engagement to seek better social and environmental performance in entire industries.[22]

Corporate engagement can also be done through a third party. Hermes Investment Management via Hermes EOS, for example, serves as a third-party engagement service for a wide variety of investors with common concerns. Because it represents the collective concerns of these investors, it represents a kind of aggregate view of how social and environmental issues impact investors systematically. Rather than divesting outright, Hermes believes that "working with firms to mitigate ESG risks—while reserving the option to sell down where a company is unable or unwilling to improve—can provide the greatest holistic benefits."[23] Hermes has increasingly started to engage companies on human rights issues, recently confronting an international construction company on the issue of managing human rights and modern slavery risks in its operations in Qatar. Consequently, the construction company conducted a human rights impact assessment and signed an agreement between the Qatar real estate company and unions covering the human rights of the workers in Qatar and the company's subcontractors.[24]

Hermes has also developed tools that enable fund managers and engagement analysts to form a holistic view of a company's climate risk. The tools provide real-time information about the level and intensity of carbon risk across portfolios, which portfolio companies are the greatest emitters, and where to target engagement activity. Hermes engages with companies exposed to climate change–related risks to improve its clients' portfolios' resilience in accordance with the recommendations by the Task Force on Climate-Related Financial Disclosures.[25] In cases such as climate change, the comprehensiveness of this approach transcends one-off engagements with individual firms to promote systemic change.

Although a systemic approach to engagement is a strategy primarily employed by institutional investors—the larger the investor, the greater the influence—individual investors can also vote their proxies, write to companies, and urge their managers to take an active role in engagement on social and environmental issues.

Adding Manager Evaluation and Selection

Manager selection involves the incorporation of investment criteria into the selection and monitoring of external vendors used to manage assets. Conventional investors commonly evaluate managers' short- and long-term financial returns, their chosen investment style and ability to stick to that style through different market conditions, and the thoroughness of their research practices. Sustainable investors add in assessments of managers' research and experience with regard to ESG risks and rewards, and the impact of these considerations, positive or negative, on managers' financial performance.[26]

In some instances, managers must ensure only that they have an established policy for dealing with ESG risks when material to specific firms; in others, the policy must meet certain standards with systemic implications. These might include encouraging managers to join industry organizations advocating system-level considerations for certain issues (e.g., the United Nations Principles for Responsible Investment's Active Ownership 2.0 initiative). Some investors select only those managers that have a documented track record of generating positive economic or social impact.[27]

For example, Aviva Investors (discussed further in chapter 5) assesses potential external managers based on their ESG integration capacity, including their engagement efforts. It maintains a "buy list" of managers that pass its various criteria for its portfolio managers to choose from. It also surveys asset managers on their ESG practices every two years. It does so in part "to raise awareness and enhance [its] understanding of best practice regarding ESG integration in the industry."[28]

Similarly, asset class teams and investment programs with CalPERS evaluate potential—and monitor existing—external managers for their incorporation of ESG factors. Teams develop and use their own evaluation processes, and questionnaires for managers incorporate questions from the United Nations Principles for Responsible Investment Reporting Framework, which CalPERS helped develop.[29]

These large institutional investors have taken an initial step toward integration of a system-related perspective into their manager selection: that of ESG integration into security selection and portfolio risk control. As the systemic nature of challenges such as climate change grow in importance for these investors and their practices transition to more comprehensively address the management of such systemic risks, their evaluations of external managers will likely follow suit.

Applying Investment Tools: Water

We used the issue of water to illustrate how to determine a system-level focus area in chapter 2. Returning to the issue, we can illustrate how investors might extend traditional investment activities to encompass a system-level focus. These key investment activities might include the following:

- Adjusting an investment beliefs statement to specify a belief that environmental system-level issues such as water have a material effect on portfolios across all asset classes
- Instructing their active managers in public equities and fixed income to include water risks in security valuation models, while simultaneously promoting best-practice criteria for these asset classes with regard to fresh water

- Instructing their real estate managers to monitor water usage in their properties and report on its materiality, while simultaneously participating in the development of standardized data disclosure guidelines for the industry
- Instructing their private equity managers to report the degree to which they believe water is a material issue for each of their investments and, when material, what policies they have in place for managing the issue, and including such reporting requirements in future manager selection for this asset class
- Developing water-related proxy voting guidelines and initiating an engagement program to address water issues as they relate to their portfolio holdings while engaging with these water companies' trade associations to develop best practices criteria for the long-term risk management of access to fresh water
- Incorporating requirements in requests for proposals that potential external managers have water-related expertise and that current managers report regularly on their management of water-related risks and rewards at both portfolio and system levels

Together, these initiatives at both the portfolio and system levels create a coherent strategy for positively impacting financial performance in both the short and long term. At the same time, these initiatives can positively impact water-related systems in ways that enhance their resiliency and increase future opportunities for wealth-creating investments.

Investors can adapt current investment practices such as these to focus on the risk management of and solutions to systemic social and environmental challenges. Since these steps involve what are essentially variations on familiar tools and techniques, the transitions for investors wanting to adopt a more systemic approach in these areas should be relatively smooth.

More ambitious and not so familiar are innovative new techniques and strategies explicitly designed to drive system-level change and now being pioneered by the most-forward-looking investors. The next chapter examines ten of these strategies. They are the final pieces of the puzzle that will enable investors to bridge the gap between their current practice and that needed to address the crucial challenges of the 21st century.

CHAPTER FIVE

Leverage Advanced Techniques

FORWARD-LOOKING INVESTORS are pioneering a wide range of techniques designed to contend with 21st century system-level challenges. Conventional and sustainable investors stop short of using these approaches or use them only sporadically. System-level investors embrace them.

The California Public Employees' Retirement System, discussed in chapter 4 for its ESG monitoring of managers and its investor beliefs statement, is among the largest pension funds in the United States and has strategically and intentionally pursued new strategies that facilitate the influence of environmental and social systems.

In 2014, for example, it adopted a set of investment beliefs that outline the relationship between ESG factors and investment risk, including specific issues like climate change. CalPERS believes that three forms of capital create value in the long term and are therefore critical to "capital formation" and the health of its funds: physical capital (environmental), human capital (social), and financial capital (governance). It includes among its human capital concerns "fair labor practices, health and safety, responsible contracting and diversity."[1] These are among the difficult-to-value factors that take investors beyond the simple price of securities, which we describe in this chapter as *evaluations*.

CalPERS also uses the techniques that we call *polity, self-organization*, and *interconnectedness*. In the realm of advocacy for effective legislation that it views as a "foundation upon which investors are given the confidence necessary to commit capital," CalPERS has testified before Congress and written to the US House of Representatives, expressing its support for legislation that improves access to capital and expands investment opportunities.[2] It has played a key role in the creation and support of organizations working to address systemic risks, including Climate Action 100+, the global alliance of investors engaging major greenhouse gas emitters, and collaborated with other pension funds in support of the Human Capital Management Coalition and other human capital-related initiatives.[3] Finally, it has worked to share data broadly with other investors in the crucial area of board diversity. Along with CalSTRS, CalPERS has created and maintained the Diverse Director DataSource database of potential candidates for investment organizations, corporations, and others seeking to add diversity to their boards of directors.[4]

CalPERS's work to build the field, influence policy, evaluate the difficult-to-quantify wealth-creating potential of broad environmental and societal systems, and coordinate with other investors to amplify its global influence on systemic issues is just one example from TIIP's analysis of one hundred asset owners and managers who intentionally use innovative techniques to leverage investment decisions for system-level goals. TIIP's analyses have identified ten such techniques to intentionally integrate system-level thinking in investing.

As shown in figure 2, these techniques can be grouped according to three broad or overarching tactics: field building, investment enhancement, and opportunity generation.[5] This chapter
illustrates these techniques in detail, providing insight into the
future practices of system-level investors. As broad categories they
also show the path forward for the practice of system-level investment: first, investors start working more collectively (field building), then they change the way they make investments (investment
enhancement), and then they create investment opportunities that
will improve systems (opportunity generation).

Figure 2. System-level investing techniques

These techniques differ from those conventional investors have historically used in that they stress collaborative actions, building shared knowledge bases, setting industry standards, and similar approaches to create a rising tide of investment opportunities for all investors. In doing so, they focus on key leverage points that can strengthen overall systems, enhance their resilience, and ensure their long-term sustainability.[6]

Field-Building Techniques

Field-building techniques pool resources for collective action. The idea is to share knowledge about the complexities of systems and align investors' goals with those of the government and other influencers of public policy. Collaborating with competitors is not a natural pivot for investors—it might feel unnatural or wrongheaded to them—but field building is essential to achieving influence at system levels.

We identify here three field-building techniques: self-organization, interconnectedness, and polity.

Self-Organization

The first field-building approach is *self-organization*. Self-organization is about creating collaborative organizational structures across the investment industry. It builds the investment community's capacity to address system-related challenges. It also strengthens the financial system's resilience. Creating industry-led organizations requires substantial commitments of time and resources from its members, and the rewards are often long term and difficult to assess.[7] But collective action is needed to shift the financial industry to a system-level approach. Since no one investor can effectively impact these complex systems, collaborative efforts help distribute the costs and risks evenly and fairly.

The work of Charly and Lisa Kleissner, founders of the KL Felicitas Foundation described in the introduction of this book, is a good example of how the technique of self-organization can be used to build for system change, taking an impact investment approach to the next level. The Kleissners both came up in Silicon Valley: early on, Charly worked with Steve Jobs at NeXT Computer before moving on to a software firm, and Lisa worked with Apple in those early days. When these companies went public, the two became millionaires. In 2000, they started to design a strategy for deploying their new wealth, carved off 30 percent of their assets to live off of, and used the rest (around $10 million) to create the KL Felicitas Foundation. With a mission to transform the global financial system for greater social and environmental impact, they've essentially "bet the farm" on impact investing.[8]

From the outset, the Kleissners have not been content to simply identify a number of impact investments united by various social and environmental themes around which to build their portfolios, as those taking a typical sustainable investment approach to impact often do. Instead, they have intentionally and methodically set about using their foundation and wealth to build the field of impact investment itself. Doing so has meant three related uses of the self-organization technique.

First they increased the number and capacity of entrepreneurs taking an impact investment approach around the world. Since 2015, they have invested in, lent to, or otherwise supported four incubators, including ones in Hawaii and Central and Eastern

Europe. In India, Dasra Social Impact provides leadership training for top managers at social service and impact investment organizations, among other services.

Second, they have supported the development of a network of impact intermediaries: an impact investment fund (Sonen Capital), an impact merchant bank (Total Impact Capital), and an innovative donor-advised and loan fund (ImpactAssets). In addition, they have provided seed capital to numerous impact funds in their earliest stages.[9]

Third, they created a group for like-minded investors called Toniic, which is a humorous nod to another impact investor organization, the Global Impact Investing Network, or GIIN. While a love of cocktails isn't a requirement for either of these groups, they do encourage 100 percent investment in impact strategies.[10]

Created in 2010, Toniic's vision is to create a global financial ecosystem working to generate positive financial and environmental returns. The community today includes over four hundred members from twenty-five different countries—investors who want to deploy their $4.5 billion in high impact investments across various asset classes.[11] Toniic offers field-building information, partnerships with industry leaders, market research, cataloging of past and future impact investment deals and funds, and everything in between. Their work has culminated in projects such as Toniic Tracer—"a platform that enables investors and issuers (funds and enterprises) to share and compare information about impact investments, including goals, performance and outcomes."[12] The Toniic Tracer powers the T100 project, "a longitudinal study of investment portfolios 100% activated towards deeper positive net impact in every asset class."[13]

Toniic's members have invested in countless projects where the results were both impact positive and financially beneficial. Take the Hadarim Fund, for example, which began building 150 residential units in Tel Aviv to create more jobs and encourage the municipality to invest more in education. The original investment was $11.5 million, but after its early success, the Hadarim Fund created a plan to double its investment.[14]

Interconnectedness

The next technique, *interconnectedness*, is about investors increasing the flow of information and communications about social, financial, and environmental systems among peers, with clients, and with the public at large. This approach recognizes the importance of a shared knowledge base to manage pooled sources of wealth creation and to avoid a "tragedy of the commons" when individuals or investors fail to communicate with each other and end up acting in their own self-interest. As a result, they behave contrary to the common good of all users by depleting or spoiling shared resources.[15]

In the competitive financial world, investors are used to keeping their cards close to the chest and want to have more information than the next person when making buy and sell decisions. What they need to realize, though, is that a certain amount of information sharing can be beneficial for all. Sharing baseline knowledge about risks and rewards means the whole financial industry will be better able to manage social, financial, and environmental system-level issues.[16]

CalPERS, for example, has compiled academic research in a database called the Sustainable Investment Research Initiative

(SIRI) Library. SIRI facilitates scholarly reviews of system-related research; convenes researchers to discuss environmental, social, and governance factors and related issues; and manages a public online database of 1,900 studies on sustainable investing.[17]

CalPERS formed SIRI in 2012. At that time, it was trying to create the organization's first investment beliefs statement on ESG issues and realized it needed more information before writing an effective statement. The result has been the adoption of system-related beliefs such as "Long-term value creation requires effective management of three forms of capital: financial, physical, and human" (belief 4) and "Risk to CalPERS is multi-faceted and not fully captured through measures such as volatility or tracking error" (belief 9).[18] SIRI identified published and working research papers of potential relevance to large, global, long-term, and multi-asset-class institutional investors. CalPERS didn't keep all this information to itself. Rather, it opened it up to help inform and advance how other investors understand and incorporate ESG issues into their own decision-making.[19]

Polity

The final field-building approach is *polity*, which creates stronger, more resilient social, financial, and environmental systems. This technique involves investors' intentional engagement in public policy debates about governmental rules and regulations that can have a positive impact on whole systems relevant to their investments. Beyond the typical lobbying for specific rule changes relating to their ability to exercise a system-oriented approach, polity is about a broad vision of encouraging tax incentives, regulatory reforms, and enforcement mechanisms that address systemic risks and rewards for investors.[20]

Polity is an approach that Steve Waygood, the chief responsible investment officer of Aviva Investors (the investment arm of the UK insurance giant Aviva referenced in chapter 4), has been practicing for the better part of two decades. Waygood began his career as a temporary receptionist at the environmental NGO World Wildlife Fund. He moved up in the organization and ended up creating its ethical finance program. His career has been devoted to answering two questions: Why does the financial system ignore climate change? And what can we do about it?[21]

These questions led him to Aviva Investors and, notably, the drafting of a sixty-page report on how international policy makers can reform capital markets to tackle climate change and encourage sustainability. The report recommends three major capital market reforms: "the provision of sustainability-oriented investment instruments; changes to the cost of capital to reflect companies' sustainability performance; and moves to get equity investors exercising their ownership rights in the cause of increased corporate sustainability."[22] He introduced the report at a United Nations event in 2014, and it has since gone on to influence the financing for the UN's Sustainable Development Goals and other policy decisions at the European Commission.[23] While this example of polity relates to climate change, this approach can be used for a system-level issue such as income inequality or financial system transparency.

Investment-Enhancement Techniques

Investment-enhancement techniques use traditional investment activities to bolster a particular social, financial, or environmental system. The goals of investment enhancement techniques are

(1) to make systems more adaptable to shocks and major disruptions, (2) to create more clarity about a system's challenges by increasing the coherence of, flow of, access to, and transparency of information about a system, (3) to connect stakeholders by establishing and adhering to policies and practices that bolster the system, and (4) to create market incentives that encourage positive changes in the stakeholders of the system.[24]

Three investment-enhancement techniques can help reach those goals: standards setting, solutions, and diversity of approach.

Standards Setting

Standards setting is an investment-enhancement technique in which system-level investors make the intentional decision to establish standards that discourage investments in industries and countries with practices that violate broadly accepted standards or norms or to contribute to the development of such standards. This technique aims to avoid crises of trust in the financial community that can arise when investors take actions that undercut system-level norms (for example, investing in companies that manufacture antipersonnel weapons or employ child and bonded labor). Standards setting lends legitimacy to financial institutions and can help strengthen their reputations and ensure their long-term viability.[25]

Before the 1970s, standards setting around industries was largely led by church groups. John Wesley, the founder of the Methodist church, got the ball rolling in the 1700s. He was an advocate of investing in the moneyed economy but not at the expense of life or health. He had a "do no harm" approach, primarily focused on not investing in alcohol or tobacco industries.[26]

Environmental activism and social justice movements emerged in the 1960s, and by the 1970s consumer protection concerns became a central focus as well. Much of this was largely due to Ralph Nader, an American consumer activist. His book *Unsafe at Any Speed* shed a light on the Corvair, a General Motors (GM) car that was found to literally be unsafe at any speed.[27] Nader went after GM, and GM went after him, having him trailed by a private detective. He sued GM for invasion of privacy, and GM ultimately settled the lawsuit for $425,000, which Nader used to found the nonprofit Public Citizen.[28]

Nader and Saul Alinsky, a community organizer, became the first shareholder activists who raised social and environmental issues at corporations' annual meetings. One of the first shareholder resolutions Nader filed was related to board diversity at GM, which led to the appointment of the Reverend Leon Sullivan, a black minister from Philadelphia. Sullivan wanted GM to get out of South Africa because of apartheid (the official government policy of discrimination on grounds of race) and GM was, at the time, the largest employer of black people in South Africa.[29]

Reverend Sullivan developed the Sullivan Principles, which concerned the conduct of companies in South Africa, specifically their labor relations, advocating the equal treatment of employees regardless of their race both within and outside the workplace. These demands directly conflicted with the official South African policies of racial segregation with its unequal rights. The Sullivan Principles became the basis for investors' determinations as to whether to divest from companies with operations in South Africa and led to US public pension funds in particular divesting from companies that remained engaged with the apartheid government. These highly publicized campaigns were part of the international pressure that ultimately forced passage of legislation ending South Africa's racial segregation practices.[30]

Investors have gone on to participate in the development of numerous similar codes for social and environmental conduct. Some focus on industries (e.g., palm oil, cocoa, apparel), others on specific issues (e.g., internet censorship, child labor). For example, Norges Bank Investment Management (NBIM), the manager for Norway's sovereign wealth fund, in consultation with its Council on Ethics, incorporates "internationally recognized standards" into its investment process. Those standards have led it to divest from companies in the tobacco and weapons industries, as well as those causing severe environmental damage.[31] In addition, in 2015, NBIM participated with the Organization for Economic Co-operation and Development standard-setting initiative relating to the extractives industry and the stability of the financial markets and has responded to various proposals for financial market regulation internationally.[32]

Solutions

Developing *solutions* to pressing problems is the next investment enhancement technique. This technique intentionally seeks to identify investments that both profit from the most pressing system-level challenges and resolve them positively. A solutions approach can fundamentally alter the nature of systems, creating alternatives with more positive dynamics and more extensive investment opportunities.[33]

Solutions-oriented approaches require a broad view of an investment and go beyond a "do no harm" mentality to actually do good. This approach is necessary because investors who focus only on their portfolios, even when those portfolios are meant to bolster a system, can unintentionally exacerbate system-level challenges.[34] An environmentally themed "water fund," for example, might focus on privatization of water supplies in a world of water scarcity without seeking to address the problem of access to water for the economically disadvantaged. In this way, not addressing the issue of access to water exacerbates the problem and creates additional harmful effects such as social unrest.[35] Or a "low-carbon" fund might invest in the promotion of nuclear power around the world without contending with the challenges of nuclear power plant safety, nuclear waste disposal, or the proliferation of nuclear weapons. So while it might help reduce emissions into the atmosphere, it could end up harming another part of the environmental system by generating more nuclear waste or creating social instability related to nuclear armament.[36]

A solutions approach seeks to resolve crucial environmental, social, and financial system-level challenges. The Dutch pension fund manager PGGM, for example, has allocated a multibillion-dollar portion of its assets to what it describes as a solutions or impact portfolio that focuses on four issues: climate change, food security, healthcare, and water.[37] As of 2018, PGGM had invested over $17 billion of the $23.5 billion it has targeted to be invested in sustainable solutions by 2020. Of this $17 billion, $1.53 billion was invested in climate change, pollution, and emissions solutions that year—producing over 11.6 million megawatt hours of renewable energy, or enough to power around 3.5 million homes for a year. Another $477 million was invested in water-scarcity solutions in 2018 alone—saving enough water to cover the average water consumption of 1.6 million residents in the Netherlands for a year. Its food security programs were also a success, with $128 million of invested capital returning 75,000 more tons of food than in previous years.[38]

Diversity of Approach

The final technique, *diversity of approach*, is investors' intentional use of a diverse range of investment tools to address complex system-level social and environmental concerns. For asset owners, this means adopting a broad variety of approaches to address single system-level challenges. For asset managers, it means creating multiple investment options for clients concerned with the systems relevant to their personal investment objectives.[39]

Conventional portfolio management tends to pursue a single solution to complex problems. But, for example, the complex dilemmas posed by climate change have no single solution. And no single intervention can, for example, ensure fair labor practices in a globalized labor market. It is not sufficient for system-level investors to focus on a single system-level technique while ignoring all others. Only by intentionally acknowledging the need for a diversity of approaches can these investors contend with the complexity of system-level issues.[40]

Adopting a diversity of approaches creates a mosaic of products and services, each with its own focus. Viewed as a whole, these products and services represent a complete picture of an issue. New Zealand Superannuation (NZ Super), a sovereign wealth pension fund in New Zealand, has used a diversity of approaches to address a single system-level challenge: climate change.[41] Its initiatives include the following:

- Transitioning of its equity portfolios to a low-carbon strategy
- Monitoring of its external managers to ensure compliance with its climate policies, implementation of climate-related risk assessments and valuation disciplines across asset classes, and integration of global-warming scenario analyses
- Integration of ESG into its investment beliefs
- Direct investments in alternative energy, sustainable agriculture, and infrastructure
- Sponsorship of financial industry research on climate-change scenarios
- Production of white papers on the topic
- Advocacy for incorporation of climate-related considerations among its peers in the sovereign wealth community
- Engagement with corporations to improve their climate-related policy
- Collaboration with other institutional investors to amplify its influence in advocating for progressive public policies and corporate action to address climate risks[42]

One such initiative was NZ Super's two-pronged approach to addressing climate change. Not only did NZ Super incorporate climate change into its asset pools, but it promoted—propagandized for it, if you will—this framework to other sovereign wealth funds. NZ Super saw the double benefit of encouraging other wealth funds to do the same.[43]

This example of the diversity of approaches technique demonstrates the multiple ways that investors can engage in system-level investing. It also shows that a variety of approaches is needed to influence a particular issue. Moreover, this diversity of approaches has led to concrete results. NZ Super has invested almost $280 million in FarmRight, which improves the environmental sustainability of rural farmland in New Zealand. It also has a large stake in New Zealand Gourmet, a high-quality fruit and vegetable producer.[44] And in the United States, NZ Super owns a 40 percent interest in Longroad Energy Holdings, a utility-scale renewable energy developer.[45]

Opportunity-Generation Techniques

Investors using opportunity-generating techniques do so with a different goal in mind: to enrich the pools of capital within a system. Opportunity-generation techniques help serve currently neglected needs; address systemic challenges at a local level; incorporate into decision-making the difficult-to-quantify overall value of social, financial, and environmental systems; and use the intended function of each investment asset class to enhance that value. These techniques generate a diversity of products, services, data, internal practices, and external opportunities, which help the system in question balance short-term priorities with the ability to adapt to changing circumstances and external shocks.[46]

The four techniques for opportunity generation are additionality, evaluations, locality, and utility.

Additionality

The technique of *additionality* is the intentional decision to invest in underserved people and address unmet environmental or social needs or markets. It addresses social inequalities and social and environmental market failures that ultimately decrease the resilience and stability of social, financial, and environmental systems.[47]

Current investment practice can misdirect investors into over-investing in parts of the economy already well served through considerations of short-term profit generation. That can contribute to boom and bust cycles. This current approach also diminishes corporations' responsibility for their workers when treating them as costs to be minimized through competitive contracting that leads to lower wages, fewer benefits, and less job security.[48] And that means a weaker social fabric for everyone.

By intentionally addressing currently neglected social and environmental capital needs that might otherwise go unfulfilled, additionality can reduce economic instabilities and promote more stable and sustainable growth. This diminishes economic inequalities and funds a mixture of enterprises that serve a broad spectrum of social purposes. In practice, additionality means cultivating new markets and filling gaps that address social and environmental needs in economies.[49]

The impact investment asset manager Bridges Fund Management, for example, targets opportunities that create jobs and improve the skills of workers such as vulnerable young people and aging populations, and promotes healthcare in historically underserved communities while emphasizing sustainable living. It has invested in companies that provide skills training for disadvantaged youth, energy services for low- and moderate-income communities, and programs that promote healthy lifestyles and obesity reduction.[50] This approach was evident in Bridges' investment in the Babington Group in 2009. The Babington Group is a UK-based firm providing apprenticeships and training courses for subjects including accounting and financial services, sales and marketing, project management, property services, IT, and more. Bridges' investment helped the Babington Group support "over 32,000 learners, helping over 3,700 formerly unemployed people to find jobs." The Babington Group "now works with over 2,100 employers to source and support talent, and in the past year trained over 1,600 16–18 year olds at risk of becoming NEET (i.e., not in education, employment, or training)." Bridges' investment in Babington reflects the concept of additionality because it helped address the large skills gap in the UK that hampered the economic recovery after the 2008 financial meltdown.[51]

Evaluations

The *evaluations* technique looks beyond quantifiable price and evaluates the potential of systems to provide the stability and predictability necessary to create a fertile field for investment opportunities. Investors typically collapse all types of value into a single price and require a short-term price-related "business case" for consideration of social, financial, or environmental system-level issues. To incorporate system-level considerations that are difficult to value, system-level investors must intentionally adopt evaluation techniques that might not be as easily quantifiable as price or making a short-term business case. These considerations call attention to sources of stability and predictability that can enhance long-term wealth creation. Expressed in terms other than price, they can serve as an effective counterbalance to the disciplines of market price.[52]

The Construction and Building Unions Superannuation (Cbus), founded in 1984, was among Australia's first industry-specific superannuation funds. Its more than 761,000 (as of 2019) members include workers, retirees, and their families from Australia's building, construction, and allied industries. Cbus believes that ESG issues can influence the stability and long-term success of its investments, integrating them to protect its solvency and meet its membership's long-term needs.[53] It recognizes that its investments are sensitive to climate change, for example.

Cbus believes that various difficult-to-value "capitals" are integral to its investment process and that it needs to go beyond just financial capital to drive long-term value creation.[54] These six capitals are financial capital, manufactured capital, human capital, intellectual capital, social and relationship capital, and natural capital. Cbus derives these capitals from the work of the International Integrated Reporting Council (IIRC), a global coalition of regulators, investors, companies, standard setters, the accounting profession, academia, and NGOs that promotes communication about value creation in corporate reporting. The core of an integrated report, according to the IIRC, is the demonstration of how the six capitals "represent all the resources and relationships organizations utilize to create value. An integrated report looks at how the activities and capabilities of an organization transform these six capitals into outcomes."[55]

The incorporation of these capitals into investment processes implies that assessments of difficult-to-value factors can go beyond today's pricing methods. Such assessments are a substantial step on the road to system-level thinking.

Locality

Another opportunity-generation technique is *locality*: the intentional decision to make investments that strengthen the environmental or social systems within a given geographic area—a city, state, region, or country. Such investments can simultaneously generate economic growth within a region and enhance its resilience and sustainability through support of interrelated enterprises. This approach seeks competitive short-term returns that also build a foundation for future investment opportunities in the long term.[56]

Using a portfolio-only lens, investors tend to focus narrowly on the short-term opportunities of stand-alone investments without due consideration for regional dynamics, trends, and opportunities. This holistic local context, fully understood, can become a source of diversified and resilient economic opportunities. Appropriate consideration of local circumstances is necessary for investments to be sustainable in today's interconnected world.[57]

These investors can use knowledge of local contexts and trends to develop forward-looking scenario analyses involving difficult-to-anticipate risks or rewards. For long-term investors, the short-term disciplines of efficiency do not always align with substantial opportunities for the creation of stable, long-term wealth generation within local contexts.[58]

The Ireland Strategic Investment Fund (ISIF), for example, describes itself as a "sovereign development fund"—different from the more traditional "sovereign wealth funds"—with the mission of accumulating assets as a "rainy day" source of revenue to supplement the nation's pension and similar state liabilities. It was launched by the Irish government in 2014 in response to the 2008 financial crisis and "to invest on a commercial basis to support economic activity and employment in Ireland." In doing so, ISIF is committed to ensuring that its investments provide additional financial support where it is otherwise lacking and that it does not displace or replicate investment efforts already underway. As of July 2018, "ISIF would focus on priorities that will support Project Ireland 2040; Regional Development, Housing, Indigenous Businesses, Climate Change and sectors adversely affected by Brexit."[59]

ISIF uses three key concepts in its investments to assess its positive impact on the local economy. It looks at the additionality of the investment, which it defines as the economic benefits to gross value added over and above gross domestic product that is likely to arise because of the investment under consideration. This is generally measured by considerations of output, profits, employment, and net export or capital expenditure. ISIF also considers displacement, which refers to instances whereby the additionality created from an investment is reduced or made smaller at the overall economy level due to a reduction in such benefits elsewhere in the economy. The last dimension is deadweight, which relates to instances whereby the economic benefits created from an investment would have been achieved in any event in the absence of intervention.[60]

Utility

Rounding out the opportunity-generation techniques is *utility*: the intentional decision to maximize the alignment of specific investments within a portfolio's asset classes with the social functions that these asset classes were designed to serve. This approach assumes that the characteristics of and market for each asset class differ because they serve distinct social functions.[61] For example, investors use public equities to actively participate in sharing in the benefits generated by large corporations, fixed income typically provides low-risk opportunities to allocate assets to a range of government initiatives that create public goods not easily served by private markets, venture capital can be used to fund new and risky ideas, and so on.[62] Utility seeks to enhance the effective functioning of asset classes within the overall financial system—a system that depends on a diversity of differently structured financial products to serve a variety of social and environmental needs. Intentional consideration of the utility of asset classes can help investors focus on goals other than simply "beating the market."[63]

This technique is explored in detail in chapter 3. The mechanism that public equity provides investors to engage large corporations, for example, affords shareowners opportunities to press for incremental changes, including those that can provide social and environmental, as well as financial, benefits. For system-level investors seeking to promote and demonstrate models for such changes across all industries in this asset class, customized, multi-industry indexes embodying those changes hold promise. Among those using this technique are the California State Teachers' Retirement System, for climate change and the transition to a low-carbon economy, and the Heron Foundation, for models of corporate support for community economic development and empowerment.

Investors seeking to use the natural focus of fixed income on the creation of public goods to tilt the financial community toward systemic change can use the flexibility of the bond market to create what amount to new asset classes within fixed income that have social or environmental purpose built into their standards. The creation of robust markets and standards for green bonds as demand for this product has grown over the past decade is an example of how a potentially fleeting fad can result in an institutionalized change within the financial system.

Investments in infrastructure lend themselves well to those wishing to bring about change within the functioning of a local economic system. Prudential Global Investment Management in its headquarters city of Newark, New Jersey, and Caisse de dépôt et placement du Québec in Montreal are examples of investors making infrastructure investments aimed at this type of systemic change.

System-Level Investing in Action: Water

Returning to the issue of water, these system-level investing techniques can help investors understand how they might develop a coherent strategy for positively impacting financial performance in both the short and long term while positively impacting water-related systems in ways that enhance their resilience and increase future opportunities for wealth-creating investments.[64] Figure 3 illustrates the types of specific uses to which each of these ten techniques might be put in that context.

Taken Together

The distinction between several of these techniques can be imprecise. The communications and collaborative endeavors of

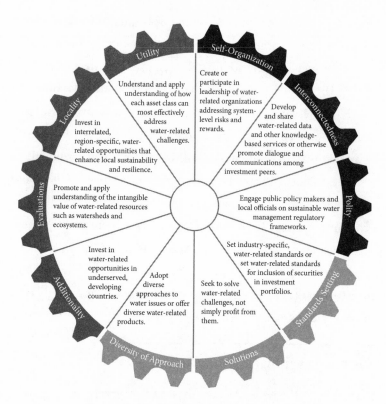

Figure 3. Techniques applied to water

interconnectedness, for example, can look much like the infra-structure building of self-organization. The environmental and social challenges addressed in a solutions approach bear a similarity to the approach of positive standards setting.

Sometimes the techniques can work well together, complementing their separate strengths, and at other times work at cross-purposes. A focus on geographic locality can often work well together with a focus on serving the unmet needs that additionality highlights. But those seeking investments that embody solutions may find the discipline of locality constraining. Some techniques might look more familiar than others to conventional investors. For large money managers, designing diverse products to accommodate clients' range of concerns about system-level issues is not that different from customizing portfolios to serve differing tolerances for risk and reward. Some of these techniques are used more often than others. We have found that those most frequently used by investors are self-organization, diversity of approach, and standards setting. This is understandable since investors have just recently started to adopt techniques of this sort, and creating peer groups and setting standards for their ongoing efforts are logical first steps.[65]

The examples in this chapter demonstrate how forward-looking investors are using new techniques to explicitly or implicitly look beyond portfolio-level considerations to the management of risks and rewards at system levels. In particular, these techniques show pathways for how investors can intentionally integrate system-related ways of thinking to varying degrees into their overall investment approaches. Through these pathways, investors bridge the gap between their daily portfolio management decision-making and their impacts at a system level.

Putting together goal setting (chapter 1) and the criteria for deciding where to focus (chapter 2), along with allocating assets (chapter 3), applying investment tools (chapter 4), and using the techniques of system-level investment from this chapter, helps an investor create a coherent strategy for managing systemic risks. It does so by impacting systems in ways that enhance their resilience and increase future opportunities for wealth-creating investments. These chapters form the core of the guidelines, investment activities, and strategies that an investor would need to implement system-level investing.

The remainder of this book addresses the difficult question of measurement (chapter 6); shows how these tools might be put into action to address one of today's most pressing systemic risks, income inequality (chapter 7); and portrays six institutional investors on the road to various aspects of a system-level approach (chapter 8).

CHAPTER SIX

Evaluate Results

THE JESSIE Smith Noyes Foundation is a family foundation with a mission of promoting social justice. As far back as the 1990s, Noyes had adopted a comprehensive program of impact investment initiatives. These went beyond simple screening out of bad actors in public equity portfolios to include program-related investments and social venture capital, with an emphasis on regenerative agriculture and community economic development.[1]

In 2016, when Noyes began a search for external managers, it faced a new challenge, one that was emerging for investors concerned with sustainability: Who among the growing number of asset managers purporting to offer sustainability products had a true commitment and deep expertise?

In issuing its request for proposals, the foundation asked typical due diligence questions around managers' experience, investment processes, and expertise, as well as their knowledge of and fluency in sustainable investing. But it also worked in questions that spoke to the ability of the manager to help facilitate the full activation of Noyes's assets "to create long-term, systemic change."[2] To this end, Noyes included the following questions: "How can our mission-aligned investment portfolio drive the creation of systemic impact in the areas of social justice, equality, human rights, health, and diversity? Are there external initiatives or targets—such as the United Nations Sustainable Development Goals (SDGs)—that might influence our portfolio?"[3]

All of which raises a number of sticky questions not just for Noyes but for all investors with system-level aspirations: How can we know which financial products and services and which asset managers are truly addressing the major systemic challenges of our times? Who is simply insulating their portfolios from the adverse impacts of ever-increasing harm to our environment and society? Who is serious about fighting climate change or income inequality versus engaging in "greenwashing" with misleading claims and empty gestures?[4]

Among other recent developments, investors' adoption of the SDGs is forcing the question of what it means to realize progress toward systemic goals. The SDGs are clearly ambitious and address challenges at the system level. As more and more managers align themselves with these goals, investors want to distinguish who is best at doing so. To make such assessments, they need a practical and comprehensive impact measurement framework—one that can separate those genuinely and effectively committed to solutions and influence at system levels from those simply protecting their portfolios against specific risks or, worse yet, from the cynical "greenwashers" of this world.

This is, in effect, a due diligence problem. Today's conventional investors have a well-established discipline for comparing the performance of one manager with another. This familiar five-part framework assesses managers' investment philosophy and their process, the financial expertise of their staff, their discipline in portfolio creation, and the financial performance of their portfolios relative to that of their peers and established benchmarks.

Because this conventional due diligence approach does not assess the social and environmental impacts of their holdings and portfolios, sustainable investors have had to confront the difficult question of how to measure that impact. Over the years, great progress has been made in addressing this challenge. See "Major Initiatives in Impact Measurement and Evaluation" for a discussion of this topic.

Today, in the course of due diligence assessments, the familiar frameworks of philosophy, process, people, portfolio, and performance as well as sustainability impact are standard. But how to incorporate due diligence when it comes to managers' skills and accomplishments as they relate to management of systemic risks and rewards remains an unanswered challenge.[5] To help address this challenge, this chapter presents a framework to help investors' track the credibility and effectiveness of managers' efforts to catalyze progress toward system-level goals.

Major Initiatives in Impact Measurement and Evaluation

For the past two decades investors have been circling around the question of what measurement and metrics can help guide them to outcomes that would take their social and environmental impacts into account. Initially, these approaches focused on metrics for corporate social responsibility (CSR). Pioneers in this area included the Global Reporting Initiative, the Sustainability

Accounting Standards Board, and corporate sustainability rating agencies like KLD Research & Analytics, Innovest (both ultimately acquired by MSCI), Vigeo Eiris (acquired by Moody's), and Sustainalytics (now part of Morningstar).

These corporate metrics have provided a useful tool in designing metrics to capture the social and environmental impact of investors' portfolios. IRIS+, for example, is a self-described "impact accounting system" with hundreds of sustainability indicators that are applicable to a portfolio's holdings and that can be rolled up to create a portfolio impact score.[6] Since 2016, Morningstar has similarly rated and ranked the impact of publicly traded equity funds. Drawing on the CSR scores of individual companies as calculated in Sustainalytics' ESG Risk Ratings framework, this method generates a score for each of the hundreds of the funds Morningstar follows and assigns a green "globe" rating by quintile.

In 2019, the International Finance Corporation (IFC) launched its Operating Principles for Impact Management to provide "a reference point against which the impact management systems of funds and institutions may be assessed." These principles are a guide for setting impact expectations, implementing investments, measuring impact against expectations, and reporting, among other things. For assessing "the expected impact of each investment, based on a systematic approach" it cites among other best practices the SMART framework often used by professional evaluators. In addition, IFC requires verification of investors' alignment with its principles. Although these impacts are of the individual investment within a portfolio, IFC has introduced a principles-oriented approach to implementation and measurement.[7]

In addition, the Impact Management Project—a global, sector-wide initiative—is developing a set of shared principles, standards, and benchmarks for defining, measuring, and reporting on impact.

These initiatives have laid the groundwork for many of the themes and recommendations presented in this chapter.

Principles, Assumptions, and a Way Forward

The best place to start in measuring and assessing system-level investments is what evaluation expert Michael Quinn Patton calls a "principles-focused evaluation."[8] Using a framework based on principles "provides guidance for making choices and decisions, is useful in setting priorities, inspires, and supports ongoing development and adaptation."[9] In addition, "Principles-focused evaluation examines (1) whether principles are clear, meaningful, and actionable, and if so, (2) whether they are actually being followed and, if so, (3) whether they are leading to desired results."[10]

From these foundations of principles-focused evaluations, investors can make sense of their managers' performance by keeping four key assumptions in mind. These assumptions are, relatively speaking, simple, straightforward, and hardly original. Together, however, they can provide a base on which to build a method that investors can use to evaluate their managers' relative performance in achieving positive, system-related, social and environmental impact.

The first assumption is that *the overall consistency of managers is essential.* Sustainable investors today tend to assume that impact can be measured solely by considering outcomes. In practice, the challenge is more complicated. Managers can undermine their outcomes achieved through unjustified claims and countervailing deeds. Consistency in managers' character, actions, and outcomes is necessary to ensure impact is sustainable.[11]

If managers tout their investments in solar or wind power, for example, as a positive outcome for contending with global warming but simultaneously invest heavily in fossil fuels because they believe that a viable economy will depend on oil, coal, and natural gas into the foreseeable future, they may be counteracting the positive outcomes they profess. Similarly, if they publicly assert that a transition to alternative energy is urgently needed but lobby for tax breaks for fossil fuels in order to benefit their portfolios' holdings, they also undermine those positive outcomes.

The second assumption is that *it is valid for investors to use qualitative judgment as well as qualitative metrics in making system-level investment decisions.* Today's managers are well trained in portfolio risk control, using quantitative data to identify pricing anomalies, opportunities to diversify risk, and effective hedging maneuvers. When systemic social and environmental risks and rewards are the challenge they face, unintended consequences are a constant danger. Judgment and the flexibility to readjust are needed to fill the void.[12]

In evaluating their managers, investors must honor the necessity for the use of judgment and then assess the quality of that judgment—a quality that, for better or worse, cannot be easily captured in quantifiable data. If, for example, investors are contending with the complex systemic challenges of income inequality—covered in chapter 7—given the systemic risks it poses to political instability around the world today, they will need to evaluate managers' judgment in how best to contend with complex contributing factors such as companies' labor, tax, and CEO compensation practices. Each involves multiple interconnected factors. To address them requires managers' judgment on how best to measure the consequences of their decisions.

Judgment with respect to systemic impacts is similarly essential in the financial realm, as Amar Bhidé points out in *A Call for Judgment*. He lays much of the blame for the 2008 crisis and near meltdown of the global financial system at the door of lenders who abandoned qualitative judgment in favor of mechanical, efficiency-motivated investment decision-making in granting risky mortgages and the poor investment judgment of pension funds, banks, and others who believed in the highly complex risk-diversification tactics used to securitize these mortgages. "Relying on case-by-case judgment does have drawbacks," he observes. "But mechanized decision-making is rarely a good alternative when the choices involve willful humans."[13]

Investors committed to achieving positive impact at system levels will need to credit judgment as well as quantitative analysis. The greater the uncertainties in the social and environmental challenges involved, the greater the need for judgment in decision-making will be.

Social and environmental systems have inherent worth is the third assumption. Many, even most, investors recognize that social and environmental systems—the stability of which they depend on for sustainable returns—have inherent worth. Because that worth is difficult to price, they tend to ignore it in their daily market-driven decisions. In doing so, they run the danger of extracting value unsustainably from these systems and undermining their long-term viability. By contrast, investors whose policies and practices incorporate these considerations support the long-term prospects and resilience of these systems.[14]

Increasingly, forward-thinking investors with long time horizons are being encouraged to recognize this inherent worth and its value to their operations. A PricewaterhouseCoopers study, for example, noted, "Sustainability initiatives do provide significant indirect sources of value" and then asked:

> How can we quantify the value created for longer-term intangible benefits? . . .
> . . . Sustainability initiatives do create *bona fide* shareholder value, but the longer-term and intangible value is a lot more difficult to quantify [than market value]. The shareholder value framework needs to be *expanded* to accommodate the value proposition of hard-to-measure initiatives, including sustainability projects (italics in the original).[15]

Investors seeking to preserve the worth of these systems need to evaluate managers' success in incorporating such considerations.

The fourth assumption is *balance is an ongoing challenge in investing.* To be sustainable, investing needs to balance the short term with the long term, the creation of private goods with those for the public, self-interest with the interests of the community, and, in practical terms, the interests of managers' portfolios with those of the systems within which they reside.[16]

When confronting systemic challenges, investors will want to look for managers who can walk balanced on two feet. They will not want managers who invest, for example, in solar and wind power simply because they can be labelled "sustainable" without also considering their business models and quality of their management. On the other hand, they should not avoid renewable energy opportunities entirely because of the unpredictability of their future prospects. Without balancing the practicalities of today with the needs of tomorrow, investors can become insolvent before the trends of tomorrow materialize or can find themselves irrelevant today because tomorrow came too soon.

Investors already engage in such balancing acts when seeking an "efficient frontier" that simultaneously maximizes the risk and reward requirements of their clients. For a holistic understanding of their system-level social and environmental impacts, investors will similarly need to evaluate the "inherent push-pull tradeoff" between short-term benefit and long-term value creation. Achieving a balance between these two lies at the crux of the achievement of stable, sustainable investment over the long term.[17]

A Framework for Evaluating System-Level Progress

Building on these four assumptions, investors can construct an assessment and measurement approach to evaluate managers' contributions to positive impacts when contending with systemic social and environmental challenges. Six fundamental questions are at its core. Answering these can help to address the larger question asked at the beginning of this chapter: How can we know which financial products and services and which asset managers are truly addressing the major systemic challenges of our times?

Question 1

Do the managers have formal beliefs or principles that are sufficiently clear, actionable, inspirational, and adaptable to be effective?

Managers should clearly state their beliefs and principles with regard to system-related social or environmental challenges. They should be able to answer questions such as the following: What is the role of the system in question in investment value creation? Does the health of that system pose material risks or offer substantial rewards? Do you believe you impact this value creation positively or negatively? Do you have a responsibility to monitor, measure, and manage these impacts?[18]

These beliefs and principles can then provide the overall guidance for evaluating managers' actions and outcomes. They can help answer this question: Have managers acted consistently with their stated beliefs, and are they likely to do so in the future? These beliefs and principles should serve as guidelines for future decision-making under varying circumstances and market conditions and help ensure consistency going forward.[19]

Managers, for example, might develop an investment beliefs statement or principles regarding the materiality of the systemic risks posed by climate change across asset classes. They might also confirm their belief in the inevitable impact, positive or negative, of their investment decision-making on climate change, their ability to manage that impact, and their responsibility to do so. Managers can state these in an IBS, investment policy statement, stand-alone sustainability report, or other forms of public reporting.[20] (See chapter 4 for more on these investment tools.)

Question 2

Can managers justify their selection of the systemic challenges they have chosen to focus on?

As covered in chapter 2, evaluating the adequacy of managers' rationale for focusing on a particular system-related social or environmental challenge can assure the investor that conflicts of interest, frivolous endeavors, or otherwise idiosyncratic, personal, or political agendas are not involved. Managers should undertake a system-related approach only in cases of broad, universally recognized systemic risks or rewards.[21]

Adequate justifications help investors understand whether managers are truly addressing systemic challenges. Without such justifications, they cannot make judgments about the appropriateness of managers' decision to focus on a particular issue.[22]

Question 3

Have the managers chosen and skillfully used techniques designed to create impact at the system level?

Only if they choose appropriately designed techniques can managers act efficiently and effectively in addressing system-related issues. Evaluating managers' choice of techniques can help investors understand whether they have sufficient knowledge to exercise influence within complex systems. If managers do not choose well or skillfully, they have little prospect for achieving impact.[23]

Properly selected and applied, these techniques can act at leverage points within a system to create impact, especially when the interests of stakeholders align with the goals of the system itself.[24] For more on choosing the right technique, see chapter 5.

Once managers have specified the techniques they have used to achieve system-level alignment, investors can judge whether these managers chose well and are properly equipped to put those chosen techniques into action.

Question 4

Have the managers applied those techniques at key leverage points within the system in ways that exercise positive influence?

To be effective, managers need to identify points of maximum leverage within a system and understand in what direction to push at those points to attain their goals. Evaluating managers' choices of key leverage points helps investors understand whether their actions are likely to exercise influence effectively and efficiently.[25]

Much of the thinking around leverage points comes from the field of systems dynamics. Developed in part in the 1950s at the Massachusetts Institute of Technology, systems dynamics is concerned with understanding the nonlinear behavior of complex systems over time using stocks, flows, feedback loops, and time delays.[26] Donella Meadows pushed the thinking further when, in 2008, she published *Thinking in Systems*, which describes the most and least effective types of interventions in a system. She outlines twelve of these intervention points, from least effective to most effective.[27]

These leverage points impact the interrelationships of the stakeholders within a system and show where intervention has the most potential for change. Investors can evaluate the appropriateness of their managers' choice of leverage points at which to intervene, as well as the ambition and intensity of that intervention.[28]

Managers who understand leverage points can see where they have the most impact and then can focus on that point. For climate change, they may engage in collaborative action with other investors or take up public advocacy or embrace communication of relevant data or reconceive market mechanisms—because each of these may be an effective leverage point for shifting current paradigms of energy production, distribution, and use.

Question 5

Have the managers' actions generated desirable outcomes?

Managers' efforts to influence systems change will be in vain if those systems fail to respond. Evaluating systems progress toward ultimate goals helps investors judge the effectiveness of managers' contributions. Three related lenses can help in this assessment: defined milestones on the road to a system that generates desirable outcomes, balance achieved among the competing systemic elements necessary for sustained change, and quantification of the specific desirable outcomes that the system overall has generated.[29]

Investors that measure managers' impact with respect to system-level change can focus on two areas. First, they can look at their managers' contributions to commitments by their peers in the investment community, along with corporations and even governments, to a common goal for system-related change—for climate risks, for example, commitment to policies consistent with the Paris Agreement on climate change.[30]

Second, investors can look at whether managers have contributed through their investments and collaborative actions to building the infrastructure needed to promote system-related change.[31] Again for climate risks, owners could evaluate managers' investments that support the creation of a physical infrastructure for renewable energy generation and consumption and, in an organizational context, the creation of collaborative initiatives to move progress ahead globally.

Question 6

How have the managers contributed to positive, paradigmatic shifts within the system itself?

Managers cannot exercise effective influence if the interests of the key stakeholders in the system in question are not aligned. Managers can impact alignment on two levels: alignment of the interests of managers among themselves and alignment of the interests of the key stakeholders within the overall system itself. Both can be difficult to achieve. Communication and the trust that it can build are key prerequisites to encouraging such alignment.[32] Managers who are successful in aligning both fellow managers and key stakeholders to address climate change will make an impact of great worth.[33]

Investors may, therefore, wish to assess how and to what degree managers' actions have contributed to an alignment of interests, for example, with respect to a transition away from a fossil-fuel-dependent economy. A single institution alone cannot create system-level change; only multiple stakeholders working together can achieve system change that will ultimately benefit everyone. Regulatory action is the quickest and most certain way of achieving such alignment, but a careful balance of regulatory action and voluntary initiatives is needed to ultimately ensure an alignment of interests throughout a complex system.[34]

Proving System-Level Progress

This process for due diligence when assessing investors' ability to manage system-level risks and rewards builds on many aspects of conventional and sustainable investment approaches. But it also differs in profound ways. It involves considerations that imply fundamental shifts in how investors think and act—shifts that are being brought to the fore in the 21st century by evolutions in our social, financial, and environmental systems. Due diligence in investment now must contend with the challenges of these developments if it too is to evolve and reflect changing times.

CHAPTER SEVEN

Case Example: Investing to Address Income Inequality

WHEN DISCUSSING system-level investing, the issue that most readily comes to mind is climate change. But investors are now recognizing that income inequality—the gap between the very wealthy and the rest of society in income and wealth—is also a system-level issue. It is of equal magnitude to climate change but with effects that are being felt more immediately. The COVID-19 pandemic made that even more obvious.

Pandemics not only have tremendous impacts on people's health and well-being, but they and associated actions or inaction by policy makers also have major economic consequences and pose very real threats to investor portfolios, financial markets, and the entire global financial system. Although investors in the United States and across the world are experiencing these threats in real time as a result of COVID-19, they and the rest of the world will not fully realize the resulting social and economic fallout and investment impacts for months (and potentially years) to come. And similar global public health emergencies will likely occur in the future. In fact, experts warn that infectious disease outbreaks will result in annual income losses of $80 billion.[1]

Pandemics such as COVID-19 are but one of the many examples of social disruptions that threaten financial systems and investment performance. A study by the Cambridge Centre for Risk Studies suggests that social unrest stemming from factors such as chronic youth unemployment—a systemic risk of increasing likelihood in the 21st century—threatens investments across asset classes.[2] COVID-19, with its ability to increase unemployment across youth workers, the gig economy, and low-income employees, is further intensifying an already existing wealth gap, particularly in the United States, and exacerbating the likelihood of social and political unrest and uncertainty for investors across all asset classes.[3]

Some amount of income inequality in and of itself is not necessarily bad—it can incentivize hard work and encourage entrepreneurship—but large income inequalities within a nation, increasingly common in the world today, can be detrimental to its society and economy. Researchers at the International Monetary Fund (IMF) found that if the income share of a country's wealthiest 20 percent of people increases by just 1 percent, GDP growth is 0.08 percent lower in the subsequent five years, whereas an increase in the income share of a country's poorest 20 percent of people is associated with 0.38 percent higher growth.[4] IMF researchers cite studies that show that prolonged periods of high income inequality have contributed to financial crises, including the 2008 financial crisis, "by intensifying leverage, overextension of credit, and a relaxation in mortgage-underwriting standards, and allowing lobbyists to push for financial deregulation."[5]

Economists Christoph Lakner and Branko Milanovic examined global income disparity between 1988 and 2008 using the Gini Index—a leading measure of global income inequality. They found that the average per capita income for the top 1 percent increased substantially between 1988 and 2008, while the gain for those at the global median was minimal. The absolute gains among the poorer percentiles were even less. Overall, 44 percent of the increase of global income between 1988 and 2008 went to the top 5 percent of the world population. Lakner and Milanovic also found that income inequality between countries has improved (i.e., more people have been lifted out of extreme poverty globally) but has gotten worse within countries (i.e., the divide between the rich and the poor has grown nationally).[6]

Greater income inequality is associated with lower output and economic growth and with decreased educational and upward mobility opportunities for poor and middle-income people, as well as more frequent and deeper economic busts. Wealth inequality also affects the politics and governments of nations. Recent years have seen a rise in nationalistic populism, trade wars, and tendencies toward isolationism. All are signs of the stresses of broad wealth inequality.[7] Elections in the United States and the United Kingdom have certainly been influenced by an increasing wealth gap; the political climates in Austria, the Netherlands, and other European countries are also feeling the strain of wealth and income inequality. It has triggered social unrest in France, Chile, Iran, and elsewhere. And ultimately, a growing gap between the haves and have-nots erodes trust in institutions—including governments—that is crucial to the stability of our global economy and financial system.

According to a 2016 report by the Principles for Responsible Investment and the Initiative for Responsible Investment, the effect of economic inequality on investors is potentially three-fold. It might (1) negatively impact long-term investment performance, (2) change the risks and opportunities that affect the universe of investment opportunities, and (3) destabilize the financial system within which investors operate—all of which threaten portfolios and bottom lines.[8] These challenges are all the more noteworthy given that investors themselves may have contributed, unwittingly or not, to the intensification of inequality.[9]

Many investors are contributing to income inequality, but some are trying to address it. One asset management group worked with a Mexican mining corporation to shore up labor relations, which led to workers making higher wages. Another impact investing firm promotes and guides investors to put their money into underserved markets, such as India and Latin America, which ultimately helps low-income people by focusing on financial services, education, agriculture, healthcare, and housing. And a coalition of institutional investors has called on the Securities and Exchange Commission to mandate companies to disclose more about their management of employee relations.

Despite the attempts some major investors are making to address income inequality, understanding how to eradicate the fundamental causes of huge wealth gaps has proven elusive. This chapter first delves into the macro-level causes of income inequality around the world and then explores how investors can use a system-level approach to reduce income inequality and its associated threats to our economy.

Income Inequality: How Did We Get Here?

In the last decades of the 20th century, massive paradigm shifts occurred in corporate and financial systems, leading to increased income inequality. A "fissuring" happened between corporations and their employees, and connections broke down between CEOs and many of their stakeholders through developments related to outsourcing of labor and increased CEO compensation. Similarly, tax avoidance schemes have weakened the connection between corporations and governments, limiting governments' ability to provide social supports and reduce inequality.

Corporate "Fissuring"

Professor David Weil, an expert in employment and labor market policy, argues in *The Fissured Workplace* that large, global firms operating in developed markets are increasingly concentrating on activities that are considered their core value drivers while contracting out noncentral work to other organizations. Weil uses the term *fissuring* to explain this common corporate approach in which what were once part of standard business functions—such as manufacturing of products or components, human resource services, or security and janitorial work—have become price-oriented services subcontracted to low-cost third-party providers. According to Weil, this fissuring, based in part on an effort to reduce costs and utilize new technologies to ensure production quality and coordination, has exacerbated an erosion in labor standards and a rise in income inequality.[10]

CEO Compensation

Similarly, over the past several decades, tying CEO compensation to stock performance has become standard practice in an effort to ensure the maximization of shareholder value. This practice has led to the skyrocketing of CEOs' total remuneration and become a highly visible symbol of the growing disparity between income for those at the apex of the pyramid and that of the rest of society. Given that in the United States alone "the top 1% own almost 40% of the stock market," it is therefore not surprising that maximization of stock price as the primary expression of value creation leads to income inequality.[11]

Researchers at the investment management firm Grantham, Mayo, Van Otterloo & Co. showed that in the period from 1949 to 1953, about 77 percent of income growth went to the bottom 90 percent of the population. In the period from 2009 to 2015, this was almost exactly reversed, with the top 10 percent getting approximately 75 percent of income growth. The authors observed that the "problem with this (aside from being an affront to any sense of fairness) is that the 90% have a much higher propensity to consume than the top 10%. Thus, as income and wealth are concentrated in the hands of fewer and fewer, growth is likely to slow significantly."[12]

Corporate Responsibility for Taxes

Corporations—with the goal of creating shareholder value, among other things—have become increasingly sophisticated in their use of transfer pricing, tax havens, and tax breaks to reduce the income taxes they pay. Figures cited by the Center on Budget and Policy Priorities show that corporate taxes used to make up a larger share of the GDP than current levels.[13] This maximization of tax avoidance drives a wedge between these corporations and the governments on which they depend for many basic services. Although many seek to minimize their payments to governments, these corporations rely on the infrastructure, judicial system, national and international security, and various social benefit programs that government can best provide.[14]

These shifts, to which the financial community has contributed, have occurred with little regard to their external costs to society or their opportunity costs for the support of basic social and environmental systems and infrastructures, as well as for stakeholders on which sustainable profits and returns ultimately depend. The remainder of this chapter focuses on how the financial community can use a system-level approach to reduce the gaps in income and bring more stability to the financial system.

Reducing Inequality: Three Legs of the Stool

Bringing about a paradigm shift that can restore the connectivity that has been lost between long-term investors, corporations, employees, and government may seem a daunting task. But just as investors shifted at the end of the 20th century to an increased emphasis on maximization of short-term returns, so too can these investors shift to a system-level focus that incorporates all stakeholders and long-term benefit maximization.

Because investors contribute to income inequality, reforms in their practice can also help alleviate it. Currently, their search for short-term returns justifies investments in companies and other opportunities that squeeze labor for profits, avoid paying taxes, and favor highly compensated CEOs and managers in their own and others' operations. Investors can bring about positive change by pushing for strong labor relations, encouraging the payment of appropriate taxes, and supporting and implementing equitable pay for CEOs and top managers. We think of these as the three legs of the stool of how investors can reduce income inequality.[15]

Improving Labor Relations

Investors can clarify expectations and engagement goals with corporations on the fair treatment of their direct and indirect workforce. By setting these standards, investors will mitigate the risks associated with fissuring and help bring greater connectivity between corporations and their employees.[16]

Data collection and availability is a critical piece in the development of these standards. Investors are, for example, supporting the data-gathering efforts of the Workforce Disclosure Initiative (WDI). The WDI advocates disclosure of data on wages, benefits, training, retention, and union relations. It was created in 2017 by a group of over one hundred institutional investors with $11.5 trillion in assets under management. The WDI encourages companies to produce standardized and detailed reporting across the whole of their employment footprint, including each company's use of part-time, temporary, and contract workers, and how it navigates and identifies risks in both its direct operations and throughout its supply chain. The WDI also asks companies to document how they use their leverage in business relationships to create strong labor standards and expectations related to the payment of living wages, robust occupational safety and health conditions, and training.[17]

With this data in place, accountability standards can be developed. Some public pension funds, for example, require responsible contractor policies (RCPs) in their real estate and infrastructure investments.[18] RCPs set labor standards in these markets, changing the model from a "race to the bottom" in a zero-sum game of cost cutting to one based on practices including fair compensation and working conditions. RCPs typically stipulate that for real estate and infrastructure projects in which it is a majority owner, the investor favors the use of contractors and subcontractors that provide fair wages and benefits and adequate training. These policies often express support for unionized contractors and union-related considerations. Among those long-term investors with formal RCPs are California Public Employees' Retirement System, New York State Common Retirement Fund, and various New York City retirement systems.[19]

RCPs can also cover janitorial services. Since 2013, institutional investors in Australia have supported the Cleaning Accountability Framework, a multistakeholder coalition of investors, unions, the Australian government's Fair Work Ombudsman department, and others. It promotes responsible contracting policies that protect the rights of workers providing cleaning services to properties owned by institutional investors.[20]

Investors have an opportunity to show leadership in how better labor practices not only are the ethically right thing to do but also improve their bottom lines. Corporations balancing investments in their workforce with the need to control costs can increase employee motivation, productivity, work quality, and retention.

In a 2012 article in the *Harvard Business Review*, Zeynep Ton noted,

> Several decades ago, there was an intense debate about whether it was possible for low-cost products to be high quality. . . . But some companies, starting with Toyota, showed that this was a false trade-off: Investing in people and processes actually drove quality up and costs down.
>
> Today many retail managers believe that there is a trade-off between investing in employees and offering the lowest prices. That, too, is false. . . . When backed up with a specific set of operating practices, investing in employees can boost customer experience and decrease costs.[21]

Ton cites as examples of success Costco, where employees make about 40 percent more than those at Walmart's Sam's Club, and Trader Joe's, where the starting salary of $40,000 to $60,000 exceeds that of some of its competitors by more than 100 percent.[22]

Regulatory actions and employee strikes can follow when basic issues of salary and benefits are ignored. From 2015 to 2018, McDonald's, for example, faced protests, strikes, and regulatory actions by workers at its franchisees in the United States and the United Kingdom related to the Fight for $15 minimum wage campaign and unionizing efforts.[23]

Encouraging Appropriate Taxation

With respect to the payment of taxes, corporations—again with the goal of maximizing shareholder value—have become increasingly sophisticated in their use of transfer pricing, tax havens, and tax breaks to reduce the income taxes they pay. As with outsourcing, minimizing tax payments allows corporate actors to avoid responsibility for providing revenues that governments need to provide the infrastructure that investors and corporations depend on.

A paradigm under which corporations and the very wealthy avoid paying taxes widens income inequality. It can simultaneously lead to a decline in governments' ability to maintain basic infrastructure and an ensuing erosion of trust in government. By pushing for more equitable tax policies and practices, investors can benefit: the corporations they invest in will not face regulatory or reputational risks from the avoidance or evasion of income taxes, the maintenance of basic infrastructure will support stable economies, and societies with a thriving middle class will fuel a consumer-based economy.[24]

Long-term investors are uniquely positioned to encourage a paradigm that demands a full public discourse on what the appropriate levels of taxation are in a given society. For example, in 2017, Norges Bank Investment Management issued a position paper on taxes. It noted, "Representatives of the investment community have . . . not generally issued expectations as to how businesses should govern and conduct their tax affairs. This may be one reason why companies and business commentators often assert that companies, through their directors, owe a fiduciary duty to their shareholders to minimize taxes."[25] Concerned that excessive short-term emphasis on allocating profits to shareholders may not be in companies' or investors' best interests, NBIM clarified its belief that "maximizing long-term value does not require aggressive tax behavior."[26] NBIM also asserted that it expects corporate boards of directors will "discourage the pursuit of aggressive tax avoidance not in shareholders' long-term interest."[27]

Put another way, while NBIM doesn't usually have anything to say about the specific level of taxes paid by the businesses in which it invests, it does want them to know that it doesn't actually expect or want them to try to get out of paying taxes. In the process, NBIM is setting the expectation that the fiduciary duty of long-term investors to manage risks includes management of the risks of overly aggressive tax avoidance.

NBIM is not alone among investors in seeking appropriate policies related to payments of taxes. Ilmarinen in Finland, Bâtirente in Canada, the Local Authority Pension Fund Forum (an investor engagement organization representing seventy-two local and public pension funds in the UK), and Amundi (the large European asset manager) have also taken up the call.[28] The setting of examples by these investors, along with their pressure on others to do the same, can help shift the tone of the debate about what is and is not appropriate when it comes to taxes and the role of corporations and the financial community.

Pushing for More Equitable CEO Pay

For the investment community, tying CEO compensation to stock performance has become standard practice to ensure the maximization of shareholder value and returns. But tying CEO compensation to stock performance implies that a CEO's responsibility is solely to benefit shareholders—and not to both shareholders and stakeholders such as employees. If long-term investors believe that the companies they invest in have additional responsibilities to other stakeholders, they must deal with the issue of CEO compensation.[29]

The current paradigm that focuses CEOs' incentives solely on benefits to stockowners drives a wedge between corporate management and their employees that not only contributes to income inequality within the firm but also becomes a highly visible symbol of that inequality more broadly in society. A paradigm that appropriately rewards shareholders and at the same time restores the connection between CEOs, employees, and other stakeholders can motivate CEOs to focus on considerations material to the long-term health of the corporation. CEOs who take a full spectrum of stakeholders into account can benefit long-term investors, as well as the company and society as a whole.[30]

Investors can support a more equitable CEO pay model that will also enhance corporate profits and their own returns. When CEO compensation incentivizes a long-term alignment of management's interests with those of employees and other stakeholders, this in turn contributes to value creation within the firm. To shift the paradigm around CEO pay, investors should encourage public policies supportive of research on appropriate CEO compensation incentive schemes, as well as support initiatives that would require the integrated disclosure of management's commitments to the full range of corporate stakeholders with traditional financial data.[31] In addition, they can set an appropriate example within their own shops.

Établissement de retraite additionnelle de la fonction publique (ERAFP) is, for example, an institutional investor that has set standards for compensation ratios between CEOs and their employees. ERAFP—the asset manager for France's public service and additional pension plan—assesses the ratios' effect on "social cohesion." To "keep differences in remuneration between managers and employees at levels that do not negatively affect the company's business or the motivation of its teams," ERAFP has set a "socially acceptable maximum amount of total remuneration" inclusive of salary, benefits, options, bonus shares, and top-up pension plan contributions at "100 times the minimum salary in force in the country in which the company's registered office is located, which in France corresponds to the national minimum wage."[32]

A sole focus on stock price and other financial indicators raises the question of whether there is any level at which CEO compensation becomes "excessive," regardless of performance. An increasing proportion of investors are beginning to vote against compensation packages even when companies have successful financial track records. According to a 2018 report by the shareholder advocacy group As You Sow, Institutional Shareholder Services (ISS) "recommended voting against 10% of the CEO pay packages at S&P 500 companies" and against thirty-eight of the one hundred companies it identified as having the most overpaid CEOs. Because its recommendations are widely followed, a no from ISS "reduces shareholder support for Say on Pay [proposals among S&P 500 companies] by 20–30% . . . depending on a company's shareholder base."[33]

Investors identified by As You Sow as actively voting against CEO pay proposals included Allianz, which was the most likely non-US mutual fund family (and third most likely fund overall) to vote against overpaid CEO packages, voting against 79 percent of CEO pay resolutions at the top one hundred most overpaid companies, and the Florida State Board of Administration, which voted against CEO pay packages at 41 percent of S&P 500 companies and 73 percent of the one hundred most overpaid companies "and provided a relatively granular explanation for these votes."[34]

Applying the Lessons to Income Inequality

What would it look like to use the tools and techniques outlined here to confront the challenges of income inequality? The causes and solutions we have shared so far may seem relatively straightforward, but how does an investor put these things into practice when confronting such a complicated issue?

Addressing income inequality, as with any system-level issue, requires long time horizons. Many institutional investors are already used to thinking about investment strategy in the context of future liabilities (pension obligations, for example) that can range thirty to fifty years in the future; similarly, individual investors often depend on their investments to support goals (retirement, for example) that will be realized far in the future. Long-term investors are likely to have a perspective sensitive to the risks of income inequality and attuned to repairing the gaps that have emerged recently in relations between companies and employees or government.

In extending their horizon, however, investors will also confront a challenge that arises frequently in considerations of system-level issues: a tension between investments managed to short-term objectives and those with the long run in view. In the case of income inequality, investors might want to invest in a company that keeps its labor costs down and taxes paid low but neglects the long-term risks of this strategy to the company and to society. At the same time, investors cannot focus solely on a firm with long-term benefits to society at the expense of returns to their funds.

To deal with this tension, investors can follow the steps outlined in this book. First, they can set a goal (chapter 1): a systematic shift away from the short-term wealth-extracting shareholder model of the corporation toward the long-term value-creation approach of the stakeholder model.

Then, they can justify their focus on this issue (chapter 2). Income inequality qualifies as worthy of a systemic approach— not only because Nobel Prize–winning economists like Joseph Stiglitz and Paul Krugman and prominent members of the investment community validate its dangers, but because these dangers will impact investors across all asset classes. Investors can also have positive influence when addressing them, and income inequality creates uncertainties so great that conventional investment techniques can't manage its risks.

Having set goals and justified their choice, investors can now confront the question of what changes they will make to how they allocate assets and in their daily practices to bring about real change (discussed in chapters 3 and 4). Their first change is to determine which of the asset classes they invest in can best address income inequality. They may now be invested in newer alternative asset classes like venture capital, hedge funds, and private equity. These can offer outsized short-term returns but little leverage for change when it comes to income inequality. Instead, the investors could consider several traditional asset classes that have a greater potential for influence. Investment in public equities provides access to the largest companies in the world. Influencing these companies could fundamentally change business norms regarding labor and taxes. Additionally, investments in government bonds can strengthen the government's role in providing safety nets to the economically precarious. Even real estate offers opportunities with its potential to support low-income housing and strong unions.

The next step can be to extend their traditional investment tools from a company focus to the broader contexts of industry and systems. To begin with, investors may already publicly state their beliefs about the efficiency of markets or the relationship of risk and reward or the materiality of social and environmental data. But for income inequality, investors can also specify their belief in the long-term value of the stability of the social systems on which they depend. Such statements can help shift the fundamental mindset of the investment community.

Next they can construct portfolios that not only deemphasize companies with histories of poor labor practices and possibly engage with a few of them but also set standards for entire industries such as footwear and apparel; for agricultural products such as cocoa, bananas, and shrimp; and on issues such as child and bonded labor.

But these changes take investors only so far. If they want fundamental change in the broader system, investors must also adopt new techniques specifically designed for system-level influence. These techniques are described in chapter 5, and we suggest three of them here to illustrate what they would look like in the case of income inequality.

One is *self-organization*. Investors are increasingly joining in coalitions to augment their influence on corporate levels, particularly around income inequality. For example, on taxes, eleven major investors joined the Principles for Responsible Investment task force on taxes, which issued a guide on the why and how of engaging with corporations on this issue.

Evaluation is another system-level investing technique investors can harness. This technique is the willingness of investors to recognize not only the market-based value of what is often referred to as human, natural, and social capitals but also their inherent worth. For too long investors have ignored this inherent worth because it was too hard to price. But dignity in the workplace provides a stability and sustainability not only to corporations and investors but to society as a whole.

The final technique to highlight in the area of income inequality is *polity*: advocating for public policies that strengthen individual companies as well as all industries. Investors have traditionally stayed out of politics, but when systemic risks endanger all their asset classes, they can no longer remain silent. Government regulation can create a level playing field on which companies can compete when it comes to issues such as setting a minimum wage, enforcing current labor laws, and closing tax loopholes.

Striking the Right Balance

In all these steps, a careful balance needs to be struck between the need for financial returns and the need to strengthen and bolster systems. This balance is found in those firms committed to employee and labor relations, paying taxes, and appropriately compensating CEOs while still controlling costs and maintaining profitability in a constantly changing world. It is a challenging task, but investors that can strike this balance in their decision-making and offer it as a model for others not only contribute to a rising tide of competitive investment opportunities for themselves but also create a stable and sustainable society for all.

Now that these steps, tools, and techniques have been laid out and applied across various system-level issues, we move toward the end of this book with a discussion in chapter 8 on how some investors are making the transition from traditional approaches to those at a system level.

CHAPTER EIGHT

Investors in Transition

THE GUARDIANS of New Zealand Superannuation (NZ Super) are not superheroes, nor do they wear capes, at least as far as we know. But NZ Super is a "super" example of how the transition to 21st century investing is taking place. NZ Super guides a government pension plan for Kiwis over the age of sixty-five, and it does so in a groundbreaking way. Over the past decade, step by careful step, it has implemented a holistic approach to managing the risks of climate change, one of the most challenging systemic risks of our time.[1]

NZ Super's use of the *diversity of approach* technique, described in chapter 5, is just one example of how investors—not only institutions but foundations, faith-based organizations, the super-rich, and the just plain well-off—are expanding the conception of what it means to be an investor in today's new, complex world. Some speak of "universal ownership," others of "stewardship" of their assets, still others of "long-term wealth creation," "impact investment," "ESG integration," and "standards setting." Some focus on the systemic risks and opportunities of climate change, others on poverty alleviation, health, employee relations, diversity, or oceans and fresh water. All are headed down the same road toward the same end: an expanded concept of the full meaning of investment in today's globalized economy.[2]

Of course, NZ Super didn't adopt this system-level approach in a day. Going from conventional and sustainable investment to the incorporation of system-level practices as well is a slow and deliberate process.

Investors Leading the Transition

In this chapter we describe how a diverse group of six investors is embarking on a transition to a system-level focus and how each is building on a major theme in sustainable investment today to incorporate a holistic approach. Each is approaching system-level investing through a different pathway.

Japan's Government Pension Investment Fund is acting as a universal owner. The Church of England Pensions Board has focused on the stewardship obligations of managing its assets. Norges Bank Investment Management emphasizes long-term value creation for future generations. The KL Felicitas Foundation focuses on building the infrastructure for impact investment in the United States and around the world. The German insurance giant Allianz thoroughly integrates ESG factors throughout its products, services, and industry. And the Rockefeller Brothers Fund sets standards publicly for whole industries to manage the systemic risks it faces.

These descriptions show how, from different points of departure, investors can find that the logical extensions of their conventional and sustainability practices lead to a system-level perspective. Taken together, these different approaches portray key elements of that perspective and provide a holistic sense of its potential. Ultimately, they illustrate the range of investors (big and small, institutional and individual) and the range of approaches required to drive large-scale systemic change. The vocabulary they use to describe their efforts differs, but all embrace the common goal of creating more resilient social, financial, and environmental systems.

Although the gap between a traditional, solely portfolio-oriented approach and one successfully integrating system-level considerations may seem formidable at times, the understanding of how to cross that divide increases daily, as investors such as these make clear.

Transition 1: Universal Ownership

The Government Pension Investment Fund (GPIF) of Japan, one of the largest pension funds in the world, is a self-identified "universal owner."[3] By this, GPIF means it is so large that it takes ownership positions in most investable assets around the world. In effect, it "owns the economy." Therefore, its fate as an investor is tied to the health of that economy. It therefore believes that taking into account ESG factors will increase its "risk-adjusted return by reducing risks" and that "the longer the investment horizon is, the greater the risk-reduction effect becomes." Not coincidentally, GPIF also describes itself as a "super long-term investor"—because it is part of a one hundred-year pension scheme.[4]

This perspective has impelled GPIF to push its extensive network of external managers to take a broad view of their responsibilities to manage ESG risks to "minimize negative externalities of corporate activities" and "to promote steady and sustainable growth of the overall capital market," which it believes will ultimately enhance its overall investment returns.[5]

GPIF is considering the implications of universal ownership not only for its own investments alone but also for other investors that are also universal owners. In March 2020, GPIF joined forces with the California State Teachers' Retirement System, and the UK-based USS Investment Management pension fund to create "Our Partnership for Sustainable Capital Markets." Its founding document concludes with its vision of the world: "With companies acting as long-term value creators and investors acting as long-term value accelerators, together [they] can keep short-termism at bay and drive sustainable economic growth for [their] customers, beneficiaries and society."[6] This focus requires a different frame of mind: one that recognizes the interconnectedness of all investments and investors with the health of the systems in which they operate.

This concept of the universal owner has found traction notably since the publication of *The Rise of Fiduciary Capitalism* in 2000.[7] It provides a bridge between risk management at a portfolio level and that at a system level because universal investors depend on the performance of the whole economy.[8] They therefore acknowledge that their long-term performance hinges on the health of the overall economy and that they must act "in such a way as to encourage sustainable economies and markets, and must act—including acting collectively—to reduce the economic risk presented by sustainability challenges."[9]

Transition 2: Stewardship

Stewardship is the responsible management of something entrusted to one's care. It is the difference between giving a favorite niece twenty dollars and telling her "Go wild!" and teaching her stewardship by asking "What will be your principles for how to spend and save this money wisely?"

Serving as stewards of their assets has found increasing traction among major institutional investors in recent years. In May 2016, for example, the International Corporate Governance Network, which represents asset owners and managers from close to fifty countries with total assets of some $54 trillion, promulgated its Global Stewardship Principles, which call on investors to "build awareness of long-term systemic threats."[10]

Active stewardship of this sort protects and enhances the value of investors' assets by encouraging social and environmental practices that support sustainable financial performance. It acknowledges an investor's ownership obligations to consider the financial implications of practices with ethical implications, thereby transcending a simple market-based "buy" and "sell" discipline.[11] Making this connection is an important characteristic of a system-level approach.

The Church of England Pensions Board is an example of a large, faith-based organization that views stewardship of its assets as an integral part of its obligations. Pursuing this broad conception of its responsibilities, it developed a Stewardship Implementation Framework that sets forth its strategies for "systemic or strategic interventions that will have a wider impact than standard corporate engagement."[12]

This type of stewardship can have true impact. When several dams of the Brazilian mining company Vale burst in a span of a few years, destroying nearby towns and killing over 250 workers and residents, the Pensions Board, which owns stock in Vale, led the creation of a coalition of investors that demanded a "new safety system to be independent of companies." As a result, Vale and other global mining companies agreed to undertake annual audits of their dams, implement new safety standards, and commit to public reporting. Unsafe dams have been closed and the families of victims compensated.[13]

In addition, the Pensions Board has taken action to address the systemic risks of climate change, creating an "open access" climate benchmarking tool to assess the preparedness of top publicly listed companies for the future low-carbon economy and taking a leadership role in investor coalitions, including the Institutional Investors Group on Climate Change and Climate Action 100+.[14]

Stewardship expands the investor's horizon line beyond just the financial to encompass a holistic care for social and environmental systems. Being a good steward means thinking about the consequences of where that $20 goes. It is a logical step for those accepting their obligations to steward and preserve the broad frameworks within which their investments take place.

Transition 3: Long-Term Value Creation

Investors focused on long-term value creation commonly look to build the strength of sustainability criteria, sustained financial quality, and the management of both current and future economic and governance opportunities and risks. This perspective provides a natural bridge to a system-level approach—one that can appeal to asset owners with long investment horizons, such as pension funds, sovereign wealth funds, and development financial institutions, along with active asset managers seeing underappreciated value in today's markets.[15]

Norges Bank Investment Management, Norway's central bank and manager of its Government Pension Fund Global, which has over $1 trillion in assets under management, is a self-described long-term investor whose mission is to "safeguard and build financial wealth for future generations."[16] NBIM believes that the operations of the companies it invests in have impact on the world around them with long-term financial consequences both for the society at large and for its own long-term returns.

As part of its strategies to promote long-term value creation for the companies that it invests in and for society more generally, it "recognize[s] a set of international standards and contribute[s] to their development." It also "aim[s] to identify long-term investment opportunities and reduce [its] exposure to unacceptable risks." These long-term goals lead it to identify companies it "choose[s] not to invest in for ethical or sustainability reasons"— for ethical reasons when international standards are violated and sustainability reasons when long-term sustainability risks are too great.[17] In 2019, it excluded four companies on ethical grounds (and revoked previous exclusions of seven). As of that time, 104 companies were also excluded because of their involvement in problematic industries, including weapons, tobacco, and coal.[18]

In addition, NBIM sets and communicates clear expectations for companies across all industries when it comes to issues posing systemic risks, including climate change, water management, children's rights, human rights, tax transparency, anticorruption, and ocean sustainability. Each year it assesses companies' performance on reporting on these issues.[19]

NBIM's approach to long-term value creation incorporates considerations of standards and long-term risks, along with the setting of clear expectations for corporate policies and practices on systemically important considerations across all industries. This approach shows how a commitment to long-term value creation can lead to system-level perspectives. For long-term investors, the further out their horizons extend, the more easily they can see how their returns depend on the health of basic social and environmental systems—and the more readily they can act. The long-term value creation lens is both a portfolio management discipline and a vehicle to align investors' interests with those of society and the environment.[20]

Transition 4: Impact Investing

Impact investing burst on the scene in the 2010s, rapidly establishing itself as a driving force in the sustainable investment world. Impact investing is commonly characterized as investment in companies, organizations, and funds to intentionally generate measurable social and environmental impact alongside financial returns. The Global Impact Investing Network and a family of related organizations have played a leading role in promoting this concept and developed tools for its implementation and measurement of its outcomes.[21]

Within that community, which has played a major role in the impact investment world, the KL Felicitas Foundation (KLF) and its founders, Charly and Lisa Kleissner, have been out front in combining the use of their investments with grant-making to increase impact in tackling social and environmental challenges. By undertaking a combination of self-organization initiatives described in chapter 5, the Kleissners have also shown how they can push the envelope of impact investment to build their overall influence within the investment community.

This is not to say that they have neglected the direct impact of their portfolios. Indeed, KLF has "bet" 99.5 percent of its $10 million portfolio on impact investments and won. Investing in organizations and funds across the asset classes of public equities, fixed income, and private equity, it has aligned virtually all its holdings with the Sustainable Development Goals. It has made loans to MA'O Organic Farms in Hawaii with its focus on food security and youth employment. It has made a private equity investment in Forestry and Agricultural Investment Management and its work with farmers in Rwanda. And it has invested in the mixed-use sustainable forestry firm Living Forests.[22]

But its ambition also includes increasing the influence of the impact investment community as a whole to make systemic change by fortifying three of its key organizational components: the number and quality of social and environmental entrepreneurs, an interrelated network of impact investment financial intermediaries, and a group of investors that are committed to the approach that shares data and best practice among themselves.

This use of field building through self-organization shows how investors can take next steps to a system-level approach.

Transition 5: ESG Integration

Another bridge from conventional to system-level investing is ESG integration, a fast-growing part of the investment landscape. It is the first of the United Nations Principles for Responsible Investment. All PRI signatories (more than three thousand as of 2020) pledge to take up this practice.[23] The PRI has published *A Practical Guide to ESG Integration for Equity Investing* to facilitate its members' efforts.[24]

Many in the asset management business currently take a narrow approach to ESG integration, confining themselves to the integration of ESG factors into traditional security selection disciplines only. This limited approach helps address portfolio risks. It avoids companies with poor governance, for example, but doesn't change the fundamental approach to investment or reduce risks at the entire system level by, for example, supporting standards for better governance overall.[25] But to truly start down the path to system-level investing, investors must expand the way they conceive of ESG integration.

That's exactly what Allianz, one of the largest insurers in the world, has done. Through its ESG Integration Framework, Allianz has committed itself to integrate environmental, social, and governance considerations systematically into its operations. With a particular emphasis on addressing the challenges of climate change, it draws on its more than $1 trillion in assets to do so in three ways—as an asset owner, a manager of others' funds, and a purveyor of insurance products.[26]

In the management of its own funds that it receives from insurance business lines (about 60 percent of its assets under management), it applies an ESG scoring system to all public equity and fixed income security selections; engages selectively with laggards to improve performance; excludes manufacturers of controversial weapons and is phasing out its investments in coal mining and coal-fired utilities; flags ESG concerns in its other asset classes such as real estate, private equity, and hedge funds; requires its external managers to integrate ESG factors; and has about 20 percent of its portfolio invested in "green" sustainability-solutions bonds, buildings, and similar products.[27]

In addition, as an insurer, Allianz integrates into its product lines offerings to help clients address environmental risks such as climate change.[28] Allianz is, for example, a specialist in insurance for the renewable energy sector. As a leader in sustainable investment among its peers, it plays a prominent role in the United Nations–affiliated Principles for Sustainable Insurance's efforts to set ESG standards for measurement and disclosure for the industry, as well as participates in public policy initiatives relating to climate change.[29]

As Allianz shows, when ESG integration is systematically implemented, it can intentionally set standards in a holistic approach to the creation of a stable world.

Transition 6: Standards Setting

Standards setting in various forms is widely used in the sustainable investment world. It is commonly characterized as the diminished investment in or total exclusion from a fund of certain sectors or companies based on specific ESG criteria. For example, some investors concerned with climate change avoid carbon-polluting firms entirely, while others overweight and underweight their holdings based on their carbon intensity.[30]

Socially responsible investors have long incorporated versions of standards setting into their practices. As far back as the 18th century, many faith-based organizations shunned companies involved in alcohol, tobacco, and gambling.[31] Since the 1970s, socially responsible investors have similarly confronted issues such as human rights (e.g., South Africa under apartheid) and the environment (e.g., nuclear power and fossil fuels).[32] A 1972 book, *The Ethical Investor*, contained a seminal description of the ethical implications and practical applications of this "do no harm" approach.[33]

When investors set standards that eliminate whole industries from their portfolios for social and environmental reasons, they make a strong statement about values. They are saying that these firms pose systemic challenges to society. Setting these standards provokes ongoing debates through which investors can forcefully make their case for the change that they see as needed.[34]

The Rockefeller Brothers Fund, a family foundation with $1.2 billion in assets as of 2020 and a long history of supporting environmental causes, announced in 2014 a two-step program to divest its fossil-fuel holdings. It immediately began reducing its exposure to coal and tar sands and undertook a study of how best to exit from other fossil-fuel firms—some of the biggest sources of carbon emissions.[35] Because of its origins in John D. Rockefeller's Standard Oil Company fortune, the foundation's decision to use its holdings in ExxonMobil—the largest of the direct descendants of Standard Oil—to highlight its concerns about the connections between fossil fuels and climate change made the news. While John D. Rockefeller would never have considered abandoning the oil business, that is exactly what some of his heirs did.[36]

As of 2020, the fund's holdings in coal and tar sands stood at less than 0.1 percent of its total portfolio, down from 1.6 percent in April 2014. In addition, it estimated its total fossil-fuel exposure at 0.9 percent, down from 6.6 percent in April 2014.[37]

Rockefeller Brothers Fund is not the only foundation to use its investments to take a stand on climate change. The McKnight Foundation, in conjunction with Mellon Capital Management, has created the Carbon Efficiency Strategy as a vehicle for investors to reduce greenhouse gas emissions. This fund excludes coal companies altogether and overweights or underweights companies depending on their efficiency in controlling greenhouse gas emissions in operations and production processes. In 2016 it also integrated a number of broad ESG factors into portfolio construction. This fund, which McKnight seeded with $100 million in 2014, is intended as a model for other institutional investors.[38]

Within the practice of standards setting lies an implicit assertion that by "doing no harm," investors can incorporate considerations of fundamental norms into their practice in ways that will strengthen the underlying social, financial, and environmental systems on which they rely.

On the Road to Systems Change

Whether through universal ownership, stewardship, long-term value creation, impact investing, ESG integration, or standards setting, each approach represents a logical extension of the concept that investment has a direct influence on the world at large. Together, they demonstrate that investing can be managed to fulfill its promise to benefit society, while amplifying efficiency and reducing risk in the future. They represent initial steps on the journey toward system-level investing.[39]

So what can an investor do as a first step tomorrow? How does an investor get started on making the transition from conventional or sustainable investing to system-level investing?

Well, the answer depends on the type of investors, the specific issues of concern, and their points of departure. The journey begins from disparate starting points, depending on whether the investor is big or small, institutional or individual. But whatever the starting point, it's in pursuit of the same goal: resilient social, financial, and environmental systems that can contend with systemic challenges of the 21st century as diverse as climate change, income inequality, and the lack of social and environmental data in the financial markets.

In the following hypothetical scenarios—based on our real-life experience analyzing and advising a range of investors—we show what a transition to system-level investing might actually look like. Of course, each starting point, challenge, and timeline will look different, but these scenarios can help investors envision the transition to system-level investing.

Scenario 1: A Pension Fund

In this scenario, a large public pension fund with $150 billion in assets under management has for some time directed its internal and external managers to integrate climate-change risks into their security selection whenever they deem them financially material. Trustees of the fund were surprised when internal managers across all industries and asset classes reported that climate risks are material. They immediately understood the implication of this development—basically, that the fund cannot diversify away its climate-change risks; there is no place to hide. They therefore concluded that the fund must take all feasible steps to minimize the long-term risk of climate change itself, rather than simply manage risks for their individual portfolios. Despite these findings, their fellow trustees, as well as their in-house investment staff, were not convinced of the need to change current practice. Indeed, having integrated ESG considerations into security valuation, they considered their job done.

So the trustees began a campaign for a systemic approach to climate change. They started with the fund's chief investment officer (CIO). They requested the CIO to commission a third-party firm to assess the material, systemic—that is, nondiversifiable—risks that climate change posed for the fund, as well as steps to contend with those risks. The study in fact showed that about 50 percent of the fund's climate-related risks were not diversifiable and that climate change was a market risk tied to the economy as a whole and hence systemic. The third-party firm also recommended modifying the fund's investment beliefs statement, proxy voting policies, and engagement with portfolio companies to reflect a system-oriented approach. After a nine-month discussion, the board adopted the study's recommendations. It imposed several conditions, including monitoring portfolio performance and cost, as well as a two-year phase-in process. Upon conclusion of the phase-in process, the trustees, emboldened by promising financial results and outcomes related to addressing climate change, began to explore other interconnected systemic societal and environmental risks in an effort to determine what, and to what extent, other issues might be having a financially material impact on the fund.

Scenario 2: A Family Office

Family offices provide another point of departure. Take the scenario of a firm that is a $3.5 billion multifamily office that historically had discouraged the incorporation of social and environmental screens. Recently, the youngest generation of the firm's largest client assumed control of their assets and highlighted a concern that global income inequality was having a negative impact on the family's desired environmental and social outcomes. They requested that the firm use the full range of the tools at its disposal to ensure that their investments at a minimum were not contributing to this increasing problem and, if possible, could exercise positive influence.

The firm staff was taken aback by this request. They first proposed a limited approach in response: act on employee relations issues—specifically, advocate for an increase in the minimum wage. Family members were disappointed and pushed the firm to expand the scope of its initiatives. After a full and frank discussion with family members, the staff decided to add freedom of association, human rights, and supply chain risks to the mix of considerations used to vet managers and construct portfolios, although some in the family wanted more. The firm also agreed to adjust its proxy voting policies for the family's funds to reflect these concerns. Over the next two years, the firm's staff cautiously implemented this program. During that time, the firm noted that the financial performance of the funds managed with these criteria did not differ significantly from that of their other portfolios. Toward the end of the second year, as the firm became more comfortable with this approach, the staff began mentioning this option to other clients and discovered unanticipated interest. Staff at the firm were ultimately able to leverage the commitment to addressing income inequality to deepen its relationships with existing clients and attract new ones—not to mention improve the stability of its investments.

Scenario 3: A Private Equity Firm

The final point of departure we'll cover here relates to a $300 million private equity fund-of-funds focused on social and environmental impact in developing markets. The firm gathers data on the social and environmental impacts of the funds in which it invests, but this is a burdensome process. Consequently, the firm has a strong interest in the development of an industry-wide private equity standard for impact reporting. Private equity as an asset class has generally lagged others in integration of ESG into its practice, and this firm decided it needed to improve data throughout the industry. After a months-long internal debate, management decided that creating a comprehensive impact measurement database on its own would be beyond its capabilities. They opted instead for promoting a collective industry data-gathering system.

To do so, in addition to allocating an in-house staff member entirely to impact data, the firm joined working groups on the integration of social and environmental principles into private equity management, such as that of the Principles for Responsible Investment. By providing leadership in this effort through its own initiatives for issues like funding research on private equity reporting and developing an award for those with best-in-class reporting of this type, the firm hoped to enhance its own reputation within the industry while benefiting industry as a whole.

Taking the First Steps

These scenarios show that investors will confront the challenges of incorporating system-level practices and perspectives in a variety of ways, whether they're a pension fund, family office, or private equity firm, or diversified financial services firms, foundations, and insurance companies. The obstacles to implementation can be substantial, and the circumstances that move these investors to take action will differ, as will the tools they choose as they move forward. Nevertheless, those incorporating system-level considerations share the common goals of minimizing the risk of social and environmental systemic crises and contributing to the health of systems that can create a rising tide of investment opportunities for all.

It is therefore not surprising that forward-looking investors—from institutions like Norges Bank to individuals like Charly and Lisa Kleissner—understand the need for an evolution in finance to build on their current practice in ways that can deal with 21st century challenges head-on. Investors making this transition are responding to the demands of current times. They are concerned not so much with what conventional investment practice does well: manage risks and rewards at a portfolio level. Rather, they seek to bridge the gap where that practice stops short. They accept responsibility for their investments' impact on the social, financial, and environmental systems of which they are a vital part.

Investors are taking their first steps toward system-level investing, regardless of their different points of departure. Sure, investors need to do a lot more to consider themselves investing at the system-level. But they should consider themselves firmly on the path if they are using the strategies outlined here in their investing practices already.

The Time to Act Is Now

THE WORLD has always been a dangerous place, but the context, scope, and scale of today's risks have changed. They are less local, more global. Melting polar ice caps, species driven to extinction, embedded social inequities, and destabilized democracies—these are harder to undo. And it seems to take global crises to prompt a change of course—to rouse us to act.

Challenges like income inequality and climate change threaten to destabilize the very fundamentals of social and environmental systems. The world was woefully unprepared for the COVID-19 pandemic and continues to be unprepared for its unpredictable long-term social and economic impacts.

These are all wake-up calls and investors need to respond: the good news is that they can prepare for and manage such systemic challenges. Investors have more power than ever not just to contend with such risks but to have positive impact at global levels. The bad news is that the hour is growing late and the time to contribute to that impact is *now*.

The path toward system-level investing will depend on who takes what actions. Some investors may start with a comprehensive plan; others may need to take incremental steps. Institutions may adopt one approach and individuals another. Some may work together and others on their own. But their processes should have the same basic six steps if they are to get from here to there and all arrive successfully at the same end point: management of the complex, interconnected risks and rewards of the 21st century.

Six Steps to System-Level Investing

What first steps can investors take without waiting for tomorrow? How can they start making the transition from conventional and sustainable investing to incorporating a system-level approach?

The six steps discussed in this book can help on that journey.

Set Goals

Investors need to be clear about goals. Whether individuals managing their own accounts or institutional investors stewarding the funds of others—whether they like it or not—investors are making systemic challenges either better or worse. And they need to be on the positive side of that equation.

Decide Where to Focus

For investors large and small, the next key step is determining which challenges are in fact worthy of a system-level approach. Each issue needs to have consensus about its importance, relevance to investors across their asset classes, effective means for investors to exercise influence, and uncertainty that cannot be dealt with by today's conventional investment strategies.

Allocate Assets

Whether individuals or institutions, investors should know the social and environmental purpose of each asset class. What role can each most effectively play in solving systemic challenges and creating opportunities for all? Investors should ensure that the holdings in their portfolios take full advantage of the purposes for which each asset class was designed.

Apply Investment Tools

Institutional investors can extend their routine practices on investment beliefs to encompass those dealing with social and environmental systems; vote proxies to exercise systemic influence; incorporate industry-wide, issue-specific criteria into active management to address systemic concerns; and create customized models that envision new approaches for indexed, passive funds. Individual investors can mimic these steps by searching out asset managers that have already implemented credible practices in these areas and are willing to integrate the specific systemic risks and opportunities on which these individuals are focused.

Leverage Advanced Techniques

Investors need to step out of their comfort zones. Institutional investors can do this by collaborating with peers and other stakeholders to apply pressure on whole industries to address systemic issues, supporting governmental regulations of the social and environmental landscape, exercising influence in aligning the interests of conflicting stakeholders within systems large and small, and creating new financial markets that solve persistent challenges, not simply profit from them. Individuals lack the opportunities for direct participation in many of these approaches but can request that the funds and pension plans in which they are participants employ these techniques themselves.

Evaluate Results

All investors should also expect more than the usual quarterly investment reports. Individuals and institutions should ask what managers have done to influence systems positively. They can evaluate managers' actual goals for a system, the actions they have taken, the changes to which they have contributed, and the progress that the system itself has made.

The Power to Make Change Is Real

Implementation is a challenge and obstacles remain. But the pathway is clear. Investors are starting to wake up to the need for a 21st century approach. And as more set off in this direction, their power to make real change will grow.

Creating the kind of influence envisioned in this book takes time. Large systems are complex, and no one investor can move them to change singlehandedly. These changes will take place through actions taken by a variety of stakeholders, of whom investors are only one representative. Multiple investors along with other stakeholders, intervening in unique ways at different points in a system, can create a mosaic picture, a collaborative vision of what that change will look like, of how the preservation and enhancement of stable, effectively functioning systems can be achieved.

Fortifying the health of the systems that underlie the market brings long-term benefit to investors, the economy, society, and the environment. It stabilizes the social and environmental systems that feel so uncertain now.

Bob Massie, the former executive director of the Coalition for Environmentally Responsible Economies, put it well when he wrote: "All around, one can start to see a dramatically new form of capitalism rising, though still largely unnoticed—a capitalism driven by the outpouring of unimaginably vast amounts of information, tamed by increasingly sophisticated tools from data science, guided by deeper and smarter questions and thus far better equipped to generate the just and sustainable economy that our planet must discover to survive."[1]

Redirecting financial strategies to drive systems change—21st century investing—is a path forward to that end.

Notes

Introduction

1. Bob Eccles, "Measuring Investors' Contributions to the Sustainable Development Goals," *Forbes*, March 11, 2018, https://www.forbes.com /sites/bobeccles/2018/03/11/measuring-investors-contributions-to-the -sustainable-development-goal/#1a72d10e3ed.

2. James Hawley and Jon Lukomnik, *The Purpose of Asset Management* (New York: Pension Insurance Corporation, 2017), 14, https: //newfinancial.org/wp-content/uploads/2018/01/The-Purpose-of -Asset-Management-working-document-Nov-2017-Final.pdf.

3. William Burckart, Steve Lydenberg, and Jessica Ziegler, *Tipping Points 2016: Summary of 50 Asset Owners' and Managers' Approaches to Investing in Global Systems* (New York: The Investment Integration Project and IRRC Institute, 2016), 13.

4. Burckart, Lydenberg, and Ziegler, 13.

5. Burckart, Lydenberg, and Ziegler, 3.

6. Lauren Debter, "Meet the Silicon Valley Alumni Trying to Change the Way We Invest," *Forbes*, November 6, 2015, https://www.forbes .com/sites/laurengensler/2015/11/06/lisa-charly-kleissner-kl -felicitas-impact-investing/#5392f95238e7.

7. The Investment Integration Project (website), home page, accessed August 10, 2020, http://www.TIIProject.com.

8. Eccles, "Measuring Investors' Contributions."

9. Mark Carney, "Inclusive Capitalism—Creating a Sense of the Systemic" (speech, Conference on Inclusive Capitalism, London, May 17, 2014).

Chapter One

1. Leo Tolstoy, *Classic Tales and Fables for Children*, ed. Robert Blaisdell, trans. Leo Wiener and Nathan Haskell Dole (Amherst, NY: Prometheus Books, 2002).

2. Steve Lydenberg, William Burckart, and Jessica Ziegler, *Effective Investing for the Long Term: Intentionality at Systems Levels* (New York: The Investment Integration Project and High Meadows Institute, 2017), 4.

3. Anthony Shorrocks, Jim Davies, and Rodrigo Lluberas, *Global Wealth Report* (Zurich: Credit Suisse Research Institute, 2019), 6.

4. William Burckart and Jessica Ziegler, *Fundamentals of Sustainable Investment: A Guide for Financial Advisors* (New York: Money Management Institute and The Investment Integration Project, 2019), 24.

5. Herman E. Daly, *Beyond Growth: The Economics of Sustainable Development* (Boston: Beacon Press, 1996), 51.

6. Steve Lydenberg, *Systems-Level Considerations and the Long-Term Investor: Definitions, Examples, and Actions* (New York: The Investment Integration Project, 2017), 14.

7. World Health Organization, *Coronavirus Disease 2019 (COVID-19) Situation Report 63*, March 23, 2020, https://www.who.int/docs /default-source/coronaviruse/situation-reports/20200323-sitrep-63 -covid-19.pdf.

8. Steve Lydenberg and William Burckart, *Assessing System-Level Investments: A Guide for Asset Owners* (New York: The Investment Integration Project, 2020), 9.

9. Ray Dalio et al., "Populism: The Phenomenon," *Bridgewater Daily Observations*, March 2017, https://properguidance.com/wp-content /uploads/2017/03/Ray-Dalio-and-Populism-1.pdf.

10. Dalio et al., 5.

11. Dalio et al., 2.

12. *Rules of the Game: An Introduction to the Standards-Related Work of the International Labour Organization* (Geneva: International Labour Organization, 2019), 10.

13. "About the Index," Access to Medicine Foundation, accessed August 31, 2020, https://accesstomedicinefoundation.org/access-to-medicine-index/about-the-index.

14. Anna Louie Sussman, "Ex-Mortgage Document Exec Pleads Guilty in 'Robo-Signing' Case," *Reuters*, November 20, 2012, https://www.reuters.com/article/robosigning-plea/ex-mortgage-document-exec-pleads-guilty-in-robo-signing-case-idUSL1E8ML0C120121121.

15. Amar Bhidé, *A Call for Judgment: Sensible Finance for a Dynamic Economy* (Oxford: Oxford University Press, 2010), 116.

16. Stephen Davis, Jon Lukomnik, and David Pitt-Watson, *What They Do with Your Money: How the Financial System Fails Us and How to Fix It* (New Haven, CT: Yale University Press 2016), 5.

17. Lydenberg, *Systems-Level Considerations*, 4.

18. M. Gardside. "Daily Global Crude Oil Demand 2006–2020," Statista, October 21, 2019, https://www.statista.com/statistics/271823/daily-global-crude-oil-demand-since-2006/.

19. Mostafa Tolba, "Green Giant: A Creator of the Successful Regime to Reduce Global Emissions Has Died," *Economist*, March 31, 2016, https://www.economist.com/science-and-technology/2016/03/31/green-giant.

20. "Ozone Layer on Track to Recovery: Success Story Should Encourage Action on Climate," UN Environment Programme, September 10, 2014, https://www.unenvironment.org/news-and-stories/press-release/ozone-layer-track-recovery-success-story-should-encourage-action.

21. Johan Rockström and Mattias Klum, *Big World Small Planet: Abundance within Planetary Boundaries* (New Haven, CT: Yale University Press, 2015), 64.

22. Simon Bell and Stephen Morse, *Sustainability Indicators: Measuring the Immeasurable?* 2nd ed. (London: Earthscan, 2008), 5.

23. Climate Action 100+, *Climate Action 100+ 2019: Progress Report*, September 2019, 6, https://climateaction100.files.wordpress.com/2019/10/progressreport2019.pdf.

24. Climate Action 100+, 7.

25. Climate Action 100+, 20.

26. Cambridge Institute for Sustainability Leadership, *Unhedgeable Risk: How Climate Change Sentiment Impacts Investment* (Cambridge: CISL, 2015), 7, https://www.cisl.cam.ac.uk/resources/publication-pdfs /unhedgeable-risk.pdf.

Chapter Two

1. Steve Lydenberg, *Systems-Level Considerations and the Long-Term Investor: Definitions, Examples, and Actions* (New York: The Investment Integration Project, 2017).

2. Lydenberg, 16.

3. Lydenberg, 6.

4. Lydenberg, 6.

5. United Nations General Assembly, *Resolution Adopted by the General Assembly on 25 September 2015*, A/RES/70/1 (October 21, 2015), 14, https://www.unfpa.org/sites/default/files/resource-pdf/Resolution _A_RES_70_1_EN.pdf.

6. "Human Development Index (HDI)," Human Development Reports, United Nations Development Programme, accessed October 9, 2020, http://hdr.undp.org/en/content/human-development-index-hdi.

7. United Nations Development Programme, "Human Development Report 2019: Beyond Income, Beyond Averages, Beyond Today— Inequalities in Human Development in the 21st Century" (New York: United Nations Development Programme, 2019), 303, http://www.hdr.undp.org/sites/default/files/hdr2019.pdf.

8. The OECD also provides a regional well-being guide that compares a region's performance on nine well-being indicators with that of other regions in the same country and throughout the OECD. "OECD Regional Well-Being: A Closer Measure of Life," OECD Regional Well-Being, accessed August 31, 2020, https://www.oecdregionalwellbeing.org.

9. United Nations General Assembly, *Resolution Adopted on 25 September 2015*, 14.

10. Lydenberg, *Systems-Level Considerations*, 6.

11. Lydenberg, 6.
12. Gary Bowman et al., *Social Unrest: Stress Test Scenario—Millennial Uprising Social Unrest Scenario* (Cambridge: University of Cambridge Centre for Risk Studies, 2014), 2, 41.
13. *Climate Risk: Technical Bulletin* (San Francisco: Sustainability Accounting Standards Board, October 2016), 1.
14. Lydenberg, *Systems-Level Considerations*, 7.
15. Lydenberg, 7.
16. Lydenberg, 8.
17. Lydenberg, 8.
18. John Maynard Keynes, *The General Theory of Employment, Interest, and Money* (Amherst, NY: Prometheus Books, 1997; New York: Harcourt, Brace & World, 1936), 155.
19. Dewi Le Bars, "Uncertainty in Sea Level Rise Projections Due to the Dependence between Contributors," *Earth's Future* 6, no. 9 (August 27, 2018): 1275–1291, https://doi.org/10.1029/2018ef000849.
20. Lydenberg, *Systems-Level Considerations*, 8.
21. United Nations World Water Assessment Programme, *The United Nations World Water Development Report 2015: Water for a Sustainable World* (Paris: UNESCO, 2015), 19.
22. United Nations, "General Assembly Adopts Resolution Recognizing Access to Clean Water, Sanitation as Human Right, by Recorded Vote of 122 in Favour, None against, 41 Abstentions," General Assembly note GA/10967, July 28, 2010, https://www.un.org/press/en/2010/ga10967.doc.htm.
23. United Nations World Water Assessment Programme, *World Water Development Report 2015*, 2.
24. See, for example, Monika Freyman et al., *An Investor Handbook for Water Risk Integration: Practices and Ideas Shared by 35 Global Investors*, Ceres, March 2015; see also Steve Lydenberg, *Systems-Level Considerations*.
25. Steve Lydenberg, William Burckart, and Jessica Ziegler, *Effective Investing for the Long Term: Intentionality at Systems Levels* (New York: The Investment Integration Project and High Meadows Institute, 2017), 24.

26. Lydenberg, Burckart, and Ziegler, *Effective Investing for the Long Term*, 24.

27. "Study: Third of Big Groundwater Basins in Distress," NASA, June 16, 2015, https://www.nasa.gov/jpl/grace/study-third-of-big-groundwater -basins-in-distress/.

28. Brook Larmer, "The Big Melt: Glaciers in the Heart of Asia Feed Its Greatest Rivers, Lifelines for Two Billion People. Now the Ice and Snow Are Diminishing," *National Geographic*, April 2010, https://www.nationalgeographic.com/magazine/2010/04/big-melt -tibetan-plateau/.

29. Eleanor Albert, "Water Clouds on the Tibetan Plateau," Council on Foreign Relations, May 9, 2016, https://www.cfr.org/backgrounder /water-clouds-tibetan-plateau.

30 Cheryl Katz, "An Epic, 500-Year Snow Fail in California's Iconic Mountains," *National Geographic*, September 14, 2015, https://www.nationalgeographic.com/news/2015/09/15914-Sierra -California-snowpack-mountains-drought-centuries/.

31. Michon Scott, "National Climate Assessment: Great Plains' Ogallala Aquifer Drying Out," NOAA Climate.gov, February 19, 2019, https://www.climate.gov/news-features/featured-images/national -climate-assessment-great-plains'-ogallala-aquifer-drying-out.

32. Lydenberg, *Systems-Level Considerations*, 18.

Chapter Three

1. For more information about Heron, visit https://www.heron.org /about-us/.

2. "A Tale of Two Tools: Financing Housing in the San Joaquin Valley," Heron Foundation, February 10, 2020, https://www.heron.org /a-tale-of-two-tools-financing-housing-in-the-san-joaquin-valley/.

3. For more information about Heron's US Community Investing Index, visit https://www.heron.org/u-s-community-investing-index/.

4. The California State Teachers' Retirement System (CalSTRS), *Green Initiative Task Force: Annual Report Ending June 30, 2019* (California: CalSTRS, 2019), 43.

5. CalSTRS, 24.

6. CalSTRS, 39.

7. CalSTRS, 18.

8. "Sustainable Investments and Climate Solutions Program," Office of the New York State Comptroller, accessed June 30, 2020, https://www.osc.state.ny.us/common-retirement-fund/sustainable -investments-and-climate-solutions-program.

9. Robert Steyer, "DiNapoli pushes 10 Companies to Cut Greenhouse Gas Emissions," *Pensions & Investments*, April 3, 2018, https://www.pionline.com/article/20180403/ONLINE/180409947 /dinapoli-pushes-10-companies-to-cut-greenhouse-gas-emissions.

10. Caisse de dépôt et placement du Québec (CDPQ), *Bringing Together Capital and Expertise: 2019 Annual Report* (Québec: CDPQ, 2019), 49.

11. CDPQ, 70.

12. CDPQ, 14.

13. CalSTRS, *Green Initiative*, 79.

14. Rikkert Scholten and Guido Moret, "Greening the Bond Market Robeco," *Robeco*, April 24, 2020, 1–3, https://www.robeco.com/en /insights/2020/04/greening-the-bond-market.html.

15. "Bank of America Issues Fifth Corporate Green Bond for $2 Billion," *Bank of America*, October 25, 2019, https://newsroom .bankofamerica.com/press-releases/environment/bank-america -issues-fifth-corporate-green-bond-2-billion.

16. "Financing the COVID-19 Response," Barclays, June 25, 2020, https://privatebank.barclays.com/news-and-insights/2020/june /financing-covid-response/.

17. Anna Georgieva and Justin Sloggett, *A Practical Guide to ESG Integration into Sovereign Debt* (London: Principles for Responsible Investment, 2019), 7.

18. Georgieva and Sloggett, 44.

19. "Country Sustainability Ranking," RobecoSAM, accessed August 11, 2020, https://www.robecosam.com/en/key-strengths/country -sustainability-ranking.html.

20. Law Library of Congress, *Laws Prohibiting Investments in Controversial Weapons* (Washington, DC: November 2016), 3, 15, 18.

21. Rainforest Action Network, *Banking on Coal Mining: US Banks' Performance against Their Policies Since 2015* (San Francisco: Rainforest Action Network, 2018), 3, https://www.ran.org/wp-content /uploads/2018/08/Banking_On_Coal_Mining_F2.pdf.

22. "Dutch Bank Bans Loans to Tobacco Industry on Health Grounds," *Guardian*, July 5, 2017, https://www.theguardian.com/world/2017/jul/06 /dutch-bank-refuses-loans-to-tobacco-industry-on-health-grounds.

23. "Creating the Future of Banking" United Nations, accessed August 11, 2020, https://www.unepfi.org/banking/bankingprinciples/.

24. "Newark—Our Best Billion-Dollar Commitment," Prudential Financial, accessed May 25, 2020, https://www.prudential.com/links/about /corporate-social-responsibility/newark/billion-dollar-commitment.

25. "Hahne's," L&M Development Partners, accessed August 22, 2020, https://lmdevpartners.com/projects/hahnes/.

26. "Newark."

Chapter Four

1. Editors of Encyclopedia Britannica, "The Riots of the Long, Hot Summer," *Encyclopaedia Britannica*, accessed May 26, 2020, https://www.britannica.com/story/the-riots-of-the-long-hot-summer.

2. "Newark—Our Best Billion-Dollar Commitment," Prudential Financial, accessed May 25, 2020, https://www.prudential.com/links/about /corporate-social-responsibility/newark/billion-dollar-commitment.

3. "Newark"; and "Profiles of Investor Systems and Related Approaches: Prudential Global Investment Management (Prudential)," The Investment Integration Project, accessed August 31, 2020, http:// resources.tiiproject.com/database.

4. "Prudential Global Investment Management."

5. "Prudential Global Investment Management."

6. Steve Lydenberg, "Investment Beliefs Statements," Hauser Center for Nonprofit Organizations at Harvard University, October 30, 2011, https://iri.hks.harvard.edu/files/iri/files/iri_investment_beliefs _statements.pdf.

7. Lydenberg.

8. Lydenberg.

9. California Public Employees' Retirement System, *Towards Sustainable Investment & Operations: Making Progress—2014 Report* (Sacramento: CalPERS, 2014), 22, https://www.calpers.ca.gov/docs /forms-publications/esg-report-2014.pdf.

10. "Sustainability Is Gathering Momentum," Mercer, August 15, 2019, https://www.mercer.com/our-thinking/wealth/sustainability-is -gathering-momentum.html.

11. Washington State Investment Board, WSIB Investment Beliefs (Olympia: WSIB, 2014), 1, https://www.sib.wa.gov/information/pdfs /db_investment_beliefs.pdf.

12. Lydenberg, "Investment Beliefs Statements."

13. William Burckart, Steve Lydenberg, and Jessica Ziegler, *Tipping Points 2016: Summary of 50 Asset Owners' and Managers' Approaches to Investing in Global Systems* (New York: The Investment Integration Project and IRRC Institute, 2016), 10.

14. Burckart, Lydenberg, and Ziegler, 10.

15. See the website of DivestInvest for a list of approximately 1,250 organizations that pledge to divest from fossil fuels and invest in renewable and alternative energies. "Commitments to DivestInvest," DivestInvest, accessed August 16, 2020, https://www.divestinvest.org /commitments/.

16. Caisse de dépôt et placement du Québec (CDPQ), *Bringing Together Capital and Expertise: 2019 Annual Report* (Québec: CDPQ, 2019).

17. CDPQ; and "Ivanhoé Cambridge Acquires Hub&Flow, a Portfolio of 17 Logistics Assets in the Main Hubs of Paris and Lyon, from The Carlyle Group," Ivanhoé Cambridge, February 05, 2020, https://www.ivanhoecambridge.com/en/news/2020/02/hub-and-flow/.

18. Tracey C. Rembert, "Tailoring Your Engagement Plan," in *21st Century Engagement: Investor Strategies for Incorporating ESG Considerations into Corporate Interactions* (BlackRock and Ceres, 2015), 9–10.

19. William Burckart and Jessica Ziegler, *Fundamentals of Sustainable Investment: A Guide for Financial Advisors* (New York: Money Management Institute and The Investment Integration Project, 2019), 24.

20. Council on Ethics, *Annual Report 2019: Sustainable Ownership through Dialogue and Engagement* (Stockholm: Swedish National Pension Funds, 2019), 10–11.

21. Council on Ethics, 3.

22. Burckart and Ziegler, *Fundamentals of Sustainable Investment*, 24.

23. Hermes Investment Management, *ESG Investing: It Still Makes You Feel Good, It Still Makes You Money* (London: Hermes Investment Management, 2016), 2, https://www.hermes-investment.com/ukw /wp-content/uploads/sites/80/2017/07/Hermes-ESG-Investing.pdf.

24. Claire Milhench, *Public Engagement Report: The Distance between Us—Crisis Management for a Global Pandemic* (London: Federated Hermes EOS, Q2 2020), 13.

25. For more information about Hermes' carbon tools, visit https://www.hermes-investment.com/us/press-centre/stewardship /hermes-turning-heat-climate-change-launch-carbon-tool/.

26. Burckart, Lydenberg, and Ziegler, *Tipping Points 2016*, 22.

27. Burckart, Lydenberg, and Ziegler, 12.

28. Burckart, Lydenberg, and Ziegler, 53.

29. Burckart, Lydenberg, and Ziegler, 74.

Chapter Five

1. California Public Employees' Retirement System (CalPERS), *CalPERS Beliefs* (Sacramento: CalPERS, 2015), 6.

2. Marcie Frost, CalPERS, letter to the majority and minority leaders of the US House of Representatives, May 17, 2018, https://www.calpers.ca.gov/docs/legislative-regulatory-letters/congress -senate-2155-financial-regulatory-reform-05-17-18.pdf.

3. "Q&A with CalPERS on Its Strong Support for Human Capital Disclosure by Public Companies," Engagement Strategies Media, accessed August 25, 2020, http://enterpriseengagement.org/Q-A-with -CalPERs-on-its-Strong-Support-for-Human-Capital-Disclosures-by -Public-Companies/.

4. "Diverse Director DataSource," CalSTRS, accessed on August 25, 2020, https://www.calstrs.com/diverse-director-datasource.

5. Steve Lydenberg and William Burckart, *Assessing System-Level Investments: A Guide for Asset Owners* (New York: The Investment Integration Project, 2020), 16.

6. Lydenberg and Burckart, 17.

7. Steve Lydenberg, William Burckart, and Jessica Ziegler, *Effective Investing for the Long Term: Intentionality at Systems Levels* (New York: The Investment Integration Project and High Meadows Institute, 2017), 19.

8. Lauren Debter, "Meet the Silicon Valley Alumni Trying to Change the Way We Invest," *Forbes*, November 6, 2015, https://www.forbes.com/sites/laurengensler/2015/11/06/lisa-charly-kleissner-kl-felicitas-impact-investing/#5392f95238e7.

9. Plum Lomax et al., *In Pursuit of Deep Impact and Market-Rate Returns: KL Felicitas' Foundation's Journey* (London: New Philanthropy Capital, 2018), 61–63.

10. Lomax, 9.

11. Toniic (website), home page, accessed August 31, 2020, https://toniic.com/.

12. "Non-profit Network Toniic Launches Impact Investing Platform," Finextra, April 2, 2020, https://www.finextra.com/pressarticle/82020/non-profit-network-toniic-launches-impact-investing-platform.

13. "Toniic Tracer," Toniic, accessed August 20, 2020, https://toniic.com/t100/.

14. Dario Parziale et al., *T100 Focus Report 2019: The Frontier of SDG Investing*, Toniic, 2019, 5, https://toniic.com/t100-focus-the-frontier-of-sdg-investing/.

15. Lydenberg and Burckart, *Assessing System-Level Investments*, 17.

16. Lydenberg and Burckart, 16.

17. For more information about SIRI, visit https://www.calpers.ca.gov/page/investments/sustainable-investments-program/esg-integration.

18. CalPERS, *CalPERS Beliefs*, 6, 10.

19. CalPERS, 10.

20. Lydenberg, Burckart, and Ziegler, *Effective Investing for the Long Term*, 17.

21. Oliver Balch, "The Disruptors: How Aviva's Steve Waygood Is Trying to Turn the Tide on Capitalism," *Ethical Corporation*, August 28, 2018,

http://www.ethicalcorp.com/disruptors-how-avivas-steve-waygood
-trying-turn-tide-capitalism.

22. Balch.

23. Balch.

24. William Burckart, Steve Lydenberg, and Jessica Ziegler, *Measuring Effectiveness: Roadmap to Assessing System-Level and SDG Investing* (New York: The Investment Integration Project, 2018), 13.

25. Burckart, Lydenberg, and Ziegler, 19.

26. Russ Rohloff, "John Wesley's Sermon 50—On the Use of Money," United Church of South Royalton, November 8, 2016, https://www .unitedchurchofsoro.org/john-wesleys-sermon-50-on-the-use-of-money/.

27. Ralph Nader, *Unsafe at Any Speed* (New York: Grossman, 1965).

28. "American Votes 2004: Candidates / Ralph Nader," CNN, accessed August 31, 2020, https://www.cnn.com/ELECTION/2004/special /president/candidates/nader.html.

29. Richard Halloran, "Nader to Press for G.M. Reform," *New York Times*, February 8, 1970, https://www.nytimes.com/1970/02/08/archives/nader -to-press-for-gm-reform-opens-a-campaign-to-make-company.html; and Molly Roth, "Sullivan Principles," *Encyclopedia of Greater Philadelphia*, 2013, https://philadelphiaencyclopedia.org/archive /sullivan-principles/.

30. Lydenberg, Burckart, and Ziegler, *Effective Investing for the Long Term*, 21.

31. For more information about NBIM's divestments, visit https://www .nbim.no/en/the-fund/responsible-investment/divestments/.

32. Petter Johnsen, "Response to the Public Consultation on the OECD Due Diligence Guidance for Responsible Business Conduct and the Due Diligence Companion," Norges Bank Investment Management, February 6, 2017, https://www.nbim.no/en/publications/consultations/2017 /response-to-the-public-consultation-on-the-oecd-due-diligence-guidance -for-responsible-business-conduct-and-the-due-diligence-companion/.

33. William Burckart, Steve Lydenberg, and Jessica Ziegler, *Central Bank and Development Finance Institution Approaches to Investing in Global Systems* (New York: The Investment Integration Project, 2017).

34. Lydenberg, Burckart, and Ziegler, *Effective Investing for the Long Term*, 7.

35. Lydenberg, Burckart, and Ziegler, 20.

36. Lydenberg, Burckart, and Ziegler, 20.

37. Lydenberg, Burckart, and Ziegler, 20.

38. PGGM, *Annual Responsible Investment Report: 2018* (Zeist, Netherlands: PGGM, 2019), 6, https://www.pggm.nl/media/ik4l34d1 /annual-responsible-investment-report_2018.pdf.

39. Burckart, Lydenberg, and Ziegler, *Measuring Effectiveness*, 33.

40. Burckart, Lydenberg, and Ziegler, 33.

41. New Zealand Superannuation Fund, *Annual Report: 2019* (Auckland: New Zealand Superannuation Fund, 2019), 54, https://www.nzsuperfund.nz/assets/documents-sys/NZ-Super-Fund -Annual-Report-2019_WEB.pdf.

42. New Zealand Superannuation Fund, 54.

43. "One Planet SWF Working Group Publish Framework on Climate Change," International Forum of Sovereign Wealth Funds, July 6, 2018, https://www.ifswf.org/general-news/one-planet-swf-working-group -publish-framework-climate-change.

44. New Zealand Superannuation Fund, *Annual Report: 2019*, 52.

45. New Zealand Superannuation Fund, 52.

46. Burckart, Lydenberg, and Ziegler, *Measuring Effectiveness*, 13.

47. Burckart, Lydenberg, and Ziegler, 19.

48. Lydenberg, Burckart, and Ziegler, *Effective Investing for the Long Term*, 12.

49. Lydenberg, Burckart, and Ziegler, 12.

50. Bridges Ventures, *Annual Impact Report 2015: The Value of Impact* (London: Bridges Ventures, 2015), 14.

51. Bridges Ventures, *Annual Impact Report 2015*, 14.

52. Lydenberg, Burckart, and Ziegler, *Effective Investing for the Long Term*, 14.

53. *Built on Trust: Cbus Annual Integrated Report 2019* (Melbourne: Cbus, 2019), 4.

54. *Built on Trust*, 36.

55. "What? The Tool for Better Reporting," International Integrated Reporting Council, accessed August 31, 2020, https://integratedreporting .org/what-the-tool-for-better-reporting.

56. Burckart, Lydenberg, and Ziegler, *Measuring Effectiveness*, 18.
57. Burckart, Lydenberg, and Ziegler, 18.
58. Burckart, Lydenberg, and Ziegler, 17.
59. "About ISIF: Flexible, Long-Term, Sovereign Investment Partner," Ireland Strategic Investment Fund, accessed October 9, 2020, https://isif.ie/about-us.
60. "Economic Impact: Irish Portfolio Economic Impact," ISIF, accessed October 9, 2020, https://isif.ie/how-we-invest/economic-impact.
61. Lydenberg, Burckart, and Ziegler, *Effective Investing for the Long Term*, 22.
62. Lydenberg, Burckart, and Ziegler, 22.
63. Lydenberg, Burckart, and Ziegler, 23.
64. A related scenario exercise is featured in a tool kit developed by the Ceres Investor Water Hub that illustrates how an institutional investor, in this case a foundation with a board of trustees, could implement a coordinated set of investment policies and practices that would seek to address and positively impact water-related risks and rewards at both portfolio and system levels. For more information, see https://www.ceres.org/resources/toolkits/investor-water-toolkit /details#driving-systems-change.
65. William Burckart, Steve Lydenberg, and Jessica Ziegler, *Tipping Points 2016: Summary of 50 Asset Owners' and Managers' Approaches to Investing in Global Systems* (New York: The Investment Integration Project and IRRC Institute, 2016), 19.

Chapter Six

1. Sonal Mahida, *Building Power Across the Impact Investment Field: Key Takeaways from Our Investment Advisor Search* (New York: Jessie Smith Noyes Foundation, 2018), https://noyes.org/wp-content/uploads/2018/10 /JessieSmithNoyesFoundationAdvisorSearchWhitePaper.pdf.
2. Mahida, 3.
3. Mahida, 19.
4. Steve Lydenberg and William Burckart, *Assessing System-Level Investments: A Guide for Asset Owners* (New York: The Investment Integration Project, 2017), 3.

5. Steve Lydenberg, William Burckart, and Jessica Ziegler, *Sustainable Investment Products and Due Diligence: Insights from Industry Experts* (New York: The Investment Integration Project and Money Management Institute, 2020).

6. IRIS+ System, "Standards," Global Impact Investment Network, accessed October 11, 2020, https://iris.thegiin.org/standards/; and "About ISIF: Flexible, Long-Term, Sovereign Investment Partner," ISIF, accessed on October 9, 2020, https://isif.ie/about-us.

7. *Investing for Impact: Operating Principles for Impact Management* (Washington, DC: International Finance Corporation, 2019), 1–2.

8. Michael Quinn Patton, *Principles-Focused Evaluations: The GUIDE* (New York: Guilford Press, 2018), 1.

9. Patton, 9.

10. Patton, 3.

11. Lydenberg and Burckart, *Assessing System-Level Investments*, 8.

12. Lydenberg and Burckart, 9.

13. Amar Bhidé, *A Call for Judgment: Sensible Finance for a Dynamic Economy* (Oxford: Oxford University Press, 2010), 44.

14. Lydenberg and Burckart, *Assessing System-Level Investments*, 10.

15. Hervé C. Kieffel, *Sustainability Valuation: An Oxymoron?* (New York: PricewaterhouseCoopers, 2012), 3, https://www.pwc.pt/pt/sustentabilidade/images/publica/sustainabilityvaluationoxymoron.pdf.

16. Lydenberg and Burckart, *Assessing System-Level Investments*, 11.

17. Lydenberg and Burckart, 11.

18. Lydenberg and Burckart, 13.

19. Lydenberg and Burckart, 13.

20. Lydenberg and Burckart, 13.

21. Lydenberg and Burckart, 14.

22. Lydenberg and Burckart, 15.

23. Lydenberg and Burckart, 15.

24. Lydenberg and Burckart, 15.

25. Lydenberg and Burckart, 16.

26. David C. Lane and John D. Sterman, "Jay Wright Forrester," in *Profiles in Operations Research: Pioneers and Innovators*, ed. Arjang A. Assad and Saul I. Gass (New York: Springer, 2016), 363–386.

27. Donella H. Meadows, *Thinking in Systems: A Primer* (White River Junction, UT: Chelsea Green, 2008), 145.

28. Lydenberg and Burckart, *Assessing System-Level Investments*, 19.

29. Lydenberg and Burckart, 21.

30. Lydenberg and Burckart, 22.

31. Lydenberg and Burckart, 22.

32. Elinor Ostrom, "Beyond Markets and States: Polycentric Governance of Complex Economic Systems," (Nobel Price lecture, Stockholm University, December 8, 2009, 431–434, https://www.nobelprize.org /uploads/2018/06/ostrom_lecture.pdf.

33. Lydenberg and Burckart, *Assessing System-Level Investments*, 19.

34. Lydenberg and Burckart, 19.

Chapter Seven

1. Victoria Y. Fan, Dean T. Jamison, and Lawrence H. Summers, "The Inclusive Cost of Pandemic Influenza Risk," *National Bureau of Economic Research* (Working Paper No. 22137, March 2016).

2. Gary Bowman et al., *Social Unrest: Stress Test Scenario—Millennial Uprising Social Unrest Scenario* (Cambridge, University of Cambridge Centre for Risk Studies, 2014), 2.

3. Kat Devlin and J. J. Moncus, "Many around the World Were Pessimistic about Inequality Even before Pandemic," Pew Research Center, August 6, 2020, https://www.pewresearch.org/fact-tank/2020/08/06/many-around -the-world-were-pessimistic-about-inequality-even-before-pandemic/.

4. Era Dabla-Norris et al., *Causes and Consequences of Income Inequality: A Global Perspective* (Washington, DC: International Monetary Fund, 2015), 7.

5. Dabla-Norris et al., *Causes and Consequences*, 8.

6. Christoph Lakner and Branko Milanovic, "Global Income Distribution: From the Fall of the Berlin Wall to the Great Recession," VoxEU, Centre for Economic Policy Research, May 27, 2014, https://voxeu.org/article/global-income-distribution-1988.

7. Steve Lydenberg et al., *Why and How Investors Can Respond to Income Inequality* (London: Principles for Responsible Investment, 2018), 10.

8. David Wood, *Discussion Paper: Why and How Might Investors Respond to Economic Inequality?* (London: Principles for Responsible Investment and Initiative for Responsible Investment, 2016), 4, http://iri.hks.harvard.edu/files/iri/files/pri_inequality_discussion_paper.pdf.

9. Lydenberg et al., *Income Inequality*, 33.

10. David Weil, *The Fissured Workplace: Why Work Became So Bad for So Many and What Can Be Done to Improve It* (Cambridge: Harvard University Press, 2014), 7–27.

11. James Montier, *The World's Dumbest Idea* (Boston: GMO, 2014), https://www.gmo.com/globalassets/articles/white-paper/2014/jm_the-worlds-dumbest-idea_12-14.pdf.

12. James Montier and Philip Pilkington, "The Deep Causes of Secular Stagnation and the Rise of Populism," Advisor Perspectives, March 27, 2017, https://www.advisorperspectives.com/commentaries/2017/03/27/the-deep-causes-of-secular-stagnation-and-the-rise-of-populism.

13. Joel Friedman, *The Decline of Corporate Income Tax Revenues* (Washington, DC: Center on Budget and Policy Priorities, 2003), https://www.cbpp.org/archiveSite/10-16-03tax.pdf.

14. Lydenberg et al., *Income Inequality*, 13.

15. Lydenberg et al., 13.

16. Lydenberg et al., 10.

17. "Workforce Disclosure Initiative," ShareAction, accessed August 31, 2020, https://shareaction.org/wdi/.

18. Lydenberg et al., *Income Inequality*, 19.

19. Lydenberg et al., 19.

20. "Cleaning Accountability Framework: Code of Conduct," Cleaning Accountability Framework, August 2016, 1, https://d3n8a8pro7vhmx.cloudfront.net/cleaningaccountability/pages/1/attachments/original/1482122597/20161219-CAF-CodeOfConduct-web1.pdf.

21. Zeynep Ton, "Why 'Good Jobs' Are Good for Retailers," *Harvard Business Review* (January–February, 2012), https://hbr.org/2012/01/why-good-jobs-are-good-for-retailers.

22. Ton.

23. Noam Scheiber, "Push to Settle McDonald's Case, a Threat to Franchise Model," *New York Times*, March 19, 2018, https://www.nytimes.com/2018/03/19/business/economy/mcdonalds-labor.html.

24. Lydenberg et al., *Income Inequality*, 27.

25. Norges Bank Investment Management, *Tax and Transparency: Expectations towards Companies* (Oslo: Norges Bank Investment Management, 2017), 2, https://www.nbim.no/contentassets/48b3ea4218 e44caab5f2a1f56992f67e/expectations-document---tax-and -transparency---norges-bank-investment-management.pdf.

26. Norges, 3.

27. Norges, 2.

28. Lydenberg et al., *Income Inequality*, 25.

29. Lydenberg et al., 30.

30. Lydenberg et al., 33.

31. Lydenberg et al., 34.

32. *Guidelines for ERAFP's Shareholder Engagement, 2018 Version* (Paris: Établissement de retraite additionnelle de la fonction publique, 2018), 34.

33. Lydenberg et al., *Income Inequality*, 31.

34. Lydenberg et al., 31. See also https://www.asyousow.org/report/the -100-most-overpaid-ceos-2019 for details on 2019 voting.

Chapter Eight

1. "Profiles of Investor Systems and Related Approaches: New Zealand Superannuation (NZ Super)," The Investment Integration Project, accessed August 31, 2020, http://resources.tiiproject.com/database.

2. William Burckart, Steve Lydenberg, and Jessica Ziegler, *Tipping Points 2016: Summary of 50 Asset Owners' and Managers' Approaches to Investing in Global Systems* (New York: The Investment Integration Project and IRRC Institute, 2016), 145.

3. Government Pension Investment Fund, *Stewardship Activities Report 2018* (Tokyo: Government Pension Investment Fund, 2018), 4.

4. Government Pension Investment Fund, 4.

5. *Stewardship Activities Report 2017* (Tokyo: Government Pension Investment Fund, February 2018), 3.

6. Government Pension Investment Fund, "Our Partnership for Sustainable Capital Markets," Government Pension Investment

Fund, press release, March 2020, https://www.gpif.go.jp/en
/investment/Our_Partnership_for_Sustainable_Capital_Markets.pdf.

7. James P. Hawley and Andrew T. Williams, *The Rise of Fiduciary Capitalism: How Institutional Investors Can Make Corporate America More Democratic* (Philadelphia: University of Pennsylvania Press, 2000).

8. Burckart, Lydenberg, and Ziegler, *Tipping Points 2016*, 10.

9. "Macro Risks: Universal Ownership," PRI, October 12, 2017, https://www.unpri.org/sdgs/the-sdgs-are-an-unavoidable-consideration -for-universal-owners/306.article.

10. "Our Members," ICGN, accessed September 25, 2020, https:// www.icgn.org/members/our-members; and International Corporate Governance Network, *ICGN Global Stewardship Principles* (London: ICGN, 2016), 19.

11. Burckart, Lydenberg, and Ziegler, *Tipping Points 2016*, 3.

12. "Stewardship and Responsible Investment," Church of England, accessed August 31, 2020, https://www.churchofengland.org/about /leadership-and-governance/church-england-pensions-board/pensions -board-investments/responsible-investment.

13. Chris Butera, "$1.3 Trillion Church-Led Pension Coalition to Pressure Mines on Dam Safety," *Chief Investment Officer*, February 1, 2019, https://www.ai-cio.com/news/1-3-trillion-church-led-pension -coalition-pressure-mines-dam-safety/.

14. "Responsible Investment," Church of England, accessed August 31, 2020, https://www.churchofengland.org/about/leadership-and -governance/church-commissioners-england/how-we-invest/responsible -investment-1; and "Investors," Climate Action 100+, accessed August 31, 2020, https://climateaction100.wordpress.com/investors/.

15. Burckart, Lydenberg, and Ziegler, *Tipping Points 2016*, 3.

16. Norges Bank Investment Management, *Responsible Investment: Government Investment Fund Global 2019* (Oslo: Norges Bank, 2019), 1.

17. Norges, 3.

18. Norges, 86.

19. Norges, 26.

20. Burckart, Lydenberg, and Ziegler, *Tipping Points 2016*, 11.

21. William Burckart and Jessica Ziegler, *Fundamentals of Sustainable Investment: A Guide for Financial Advisors* (New York: Money Management Institute and The Investment Integration Project, 2019), 78.

22. Plum Lomax et al., *In Pursuit of Deep Impact and Market-Rate Returns: KL Felicitas' Foundation's Journey* (London: New Philanthropy Capital, 2018), 74–77.

23. "About the PRI," accessed August 31, 2020, PRI, https://www.unpri .org/pri/about-the-pri.

24. Justin Sloggett, *A Practical Guide to ESG Integration for Equity Investing* (London: Principles for Responsible Investment, 2016).

25. Burckart, Lydenberg, and Ziegler, *Tipping Points 2016*, 10.

26. *Collaborating for a Sustainable Future: Allianz Group Sustainability Report 2019* (Munich: Allianz Group, 2020), https://www.allianz .com/content/dam/onemarketing/azcom/Allianz_com/sustainability /documents/Allianz_Group_Sustainability_Report_2019-web.pdf.

27. *Collaborating for a Sustainable Future*, 34.

28. Burckart, Lydenberg, and Ziegler, *Tipping Points 2016*, 43.

29. "Sustainable Insurance," Allianz SE, accessed August 31, 2020, https://www.allianz.com/en/sustainability/business-integration /sustainable-insurance.html.

30. Burckart, Lydenberg, and Ziegler, *Tipping Points 2016*, 11.

31. Burckart, Lydenberg, and Ziegler, 11–12.

32. Burckart, Lydenberg, and Ziegler, 12.

33. John G. Simon, Jon P. Gunnemann, and Charles W. Powers, *The Ethical Investor* (New Haven: Yale University Press, 1972).

34. Burckart, Lydenberg, and Ziegler, *Tipping Points 2016*, 17.

35. Steven Godeke and William Burckart, "Impact Investing Can Help Foundations Avoid Obsolescence," *Chronicle of Philanthropy*, March 18, 2015, https://www.philanthropy.com/article/Opinion-Impact-Investing -Can/228569.

36. Godeke and Burckart.

37. "Fossil Fuel Divestment," Rockefeller Brothers Fund, accessed August 31, 2020, https://www.rbf.org/mission-aligned-investing/divestment.

38. "Mellon Capital Management: Carbon Efficiency Strategy," McKnight Foundation, accessed August 31, 2020, https://www.mcknight.org /impact-investment/mellon-capital-management-carbon-efficiency-strategy/.

39. Burckart, Lydenberg, and Ziegler, *Tipping Points 2016.*

Conclusion

1. Massie, Bob, "Welcome to the ESG Evolution," *Institutional Investor,* March 9, 2016, https://www.institutionalinvestor.com/article /b14z9q0wwhwns8/welcome-to-the-esg-evolution#.WCMlCHeZOqA.

Acknowledgments

AN EFFORT of this magnitude is the work of many, not just the names on the cover. Thus, the authors would like to thank five groups of contributors to their work that underpinned this book and that without which this ship might have run aground.

First up is the group of folks and institutions that made this book—and the authors' company The Investment Integration Project (TIIP) more generally—possible. At the top of this list is the High Meadows Institute (HMI), which provided encouragement, insights, and fellowships to the authors. Chris Pinney, the CEO and president of the board of HMI, should be particularly applauded for his patience in the face of slipped deadlines, bold proposals, and generally being game to keep placing bets on the authors, even when some haven't paid off as fast or in quite the way he might have envisioned.

The authors want to specifically thank Jessica Ziegler, TIIP's head of research. Jessica joined TIIP in the early days after the authors somehow managed to persuade her to leave a well-respected, leading program evaluation firm for a ragtag startup. She has gone on to have a hand in nearly every research project, consulting engagement, and piece of thought leadership TIIP has produced. Her name could have just as easily joined the authors on the cover.

Jon Lukomnik, managing partner of Sinclair Capital and the former executive director of Investor Responsibility Research Center Institute, has also partnered with the authors on the production of multiple TIIP projects. Jon has offered an invaluable sounding board for the TIIP team over the years—his recommendations and sage counsel having served to help the authors strengthen their better ideas and abandon their weaker ones.

Carole Laible and Amy Domini of Domini Impact Investments have generously supported the work of the authors, for which we are deeply thankful. In particular, we greatly appreciate Carole's time, perspective, and partnership. She has, in turn, shaped Domini into a true, system-level investor. The authors' collaboration with Carole, and her willingness to let the authors stress test their latest thinking within the walls of Domini, has yielded some of TIIP's biggest breakthroughs. Unsurprisingly, Carole herself has become one of the leading ambassadors of this movement.

Rounding out this initial group are TIIP's first champions: Jeb Brooks and Cherie Wendelken. As TIIP's seed investors, Jeb and Cherie put much-needed wind in the sails, enabling the authors to begin the voyage. Ever since, they have offered a lifeline to the authors on all things big and trivial, providing sound advice when asked and straight talk when needed.

The second group is the many investors and managers that the authors have advised, profiled, and featured in their research over the years. In many cases these investors took time from their busy schedules to complete surveys, attend convenings, and engage in any number of phone calls, email exchanges, and meetings as the authors fine-tuned their thinking about system-level investing.

The third group the authors would like to express their utmost gratitude to is the brain trust of practitioners and experts that have helped establish and refine the concept of system-level investing and make it more practical and useful to the field. They include Monique Aiken, Geeta Aiyer, Cambria Allen, Ian Banks, Bill Baue, Adam Bendell, David Blood, Noel Pacarro Brown, Suzanna Buck, Johnathan Burnham, Jamie Butterworth, Fred Carden, Kelly Christoudoulou, Mackenzie Clark, Scott Connolly, Avi Deutsch, Robert Eccles, Linda Eling-Lee, Paul Ellis, Allan Emkin, David Erickson, Nathan Fabian, Caroline Flammer, Rodney Foxworth, Monika Freyman, Amir Ghandar, Jeff Gitterman, Steve Godeke, Kelly Major Green, Michael Greis, Randy Gunn, James Hawley, Michael Jantzi, Kirsty Jenkinson, Isaac Khurgel, Charly Kleissner, Lisa Kleissner, Corey Klemmer, Thomas Kochan, Lloyd Kurtz, Rob Lake, Maria Mahl, Priya Mathur, Madeleine McCarroll, Meredith Miller, Bhakti Mirchandani, Wilhelm Mohn, Will Morgan, David Mowat, Michael Musuraca, Katherine Ng, Ian Nolan, Stephen Olsen, Matt Orsagh, Glenn Page, Philip Palanza, Michael Quinn Patton, Susheela Peres da Costa, Craig Pfeiffer, Gary Pivo, Bettina Reinboth, Fiona Reynolds, Nick Robins, Jean Rogers, Shannon Rohan, Delilah Rothenberg, Andrew Shannon, Anne Simpson, Mark Sloss, Anna Snider, Rene Swart, Brian Tomlinson, Lily Trager, Brian Trelstad, Xander den Uyl, Jackie Vanderbrug, Dan Viederman, Steve Waddell, Sandra Waddock, Brett Wayman, David Weil, Allen White, Tim Williams, David Wood, Amanda Young, and Jay Youngdhal. You inspired and pushed back in equal measures, for which the authors are incredibly fortunate.

The fourth group is the team of researchers, writers, editors, and designers at Berrett-Koehler (BK) Publishers and TIIP that helped build and provision this ship and keep it from running aground when the waters got choppy. Steve Piersanti, the founder of BK, captained this manuscript from start to finish. Steve kept the book from simply being a rote retelling of system-level investing key concepts and examples and instead got the authors to dig in and break new ground. Supporting Steve's efforts were Jeevan Sivasubramaniam, Simon J. Blattner, Canyon Bosler, and Julie Morse—each providing perspective on how to make the manuscript stronger. Maria Luisa Tucker and Jeff Raderstrong each became indispensable utility players, helping the authors make the prose and messaging more digestible and coherent as well as editing with the surgical precision of a scalpel, as well as with the bluntness of a hammer, depending on what was needed. JR Bascom supported the authors in the homestretch of production, helping them with research, manuscript prep, and good humor—all of which were needed as the finish line came into view. Robert Dannhauser and Mirtha Kastrapeli, longtime advisors to the authors, reviewed the first draft of the manuscript. Their feedback helped shine a light on what was working, what wasn't, and what was needed to navigate more fully to the better side of that equation.

Lastly, the authors want to thank their families and friends for all of their encouragement and support. An undertaking like this is hard enough in stable times, let alone during a global pandemic. The endless hours spent on the phone, on Zoom, texting, and emailing served to give the authors the digital pats on the back and virtual hand-holding they needed when the opportunity for the in-person versions went away.

The authors have undoubtedly forgot any number of names that should appear on this list. For that they offer their deepest apologies and gratitude.

Index

Page references followed by *f* indicate an illustrated figure; those followed by *t* indicate a table.

ABN AMRO, 66
Access to Medicine Index, 31
Active Ownership 2.0 initiative (PRI), 82
additionality technique, 89*f*, 102–104
advanced investment techniques
  application to fresh water issue, 109,
    110*f*
  CalPERS's successful leveraging of,
    87–88, 93–94
  field-building, 89*f*, 90–93, 145–146, 157
  investment-enhancement, 89*f*, 95–102,
    149–150
  opportunity-generation, 89*f*, 102–109,
    146
  system-level investing by leveraging,
    18*t*, 20, 87, 124–125, 171–172
AeroFarms, 70
AES Corporation, 37
Alinsky, Saul, 97
Allianz (Germany), 142–143, 150, 158–159
allocating assets. *See* asset classes
Amundi (EU), 140
Annan, Kofi, 34
antibiotics (animal feedstock), 42
anticorruption, 156
apartheid (South Africa), 97–98, 160
AP pension funds' Council on Ethics
  (Sweden), 79–80
Apple, 91
aquifers and glaciers, 51
asset classes
  allocation of, 17*t*, 19–20, 53–70, 171
  bonds, 55, 62–64
  fixed income, 55, 62
  Heron Foundation's use of, 53–54, 58
  infrastructure, 55, 69–70

loans, 55, 65–67
  marginally using cash as an, 55, 67
  private equities, 55, 58–60
  public equities, 55, 56–58
  real estate, 55, 67–69
  sovereign debt, 55, 64–65
  system-level change using, 54–55
  targeted to leverage points, 70
  venture capital, 55, 61
  See also portfolios
asset resources
  benefits of promoting equal access to,
    31, 38–39
  fresh water, 48, 50–51, 83–85, 99, 109,
    110*f*
  population growth and limited, 28
  stability and efficient allocation of,
    28–29
As You Sow's Institutional Shareholder
  Services (ISS), 142
Australia
  AustralianSuper, 37
  Cleaning Accountability Framework,
    137
  Fair Work Ombudsman, 137
AustralianSuper, 37
Aviva Investors, 82, 95

Babington Group, 104
balance
  assumed to be an ongoing investing
    challenge, 120–121
  between financial returns vs. strength-
    ening systems, 146–147
Bank of America (BoA), 63–64, 66
Bank of England, 16

Bâtirente (Canada), 140
beliefs. *See* investment beliefs
Beneficial State Bank, 67
Better Life Index (OECD), 44
Bhidé, Amar, 32, 119
Big Oven, The (Tolstoy), 23
bonds, 55, 62–64
Brexit, 107
Bridges Fund Management, 103–104
Burckart, William, 15

Caisse de dépôt et placement du Québec
    (CDPQ), 59–60, 77–78, 109
California Health Facilities Financing
    Authority, 53–54
California Public Employees' Retirement
    System (CalPERS), 37, 68, 75, 83,
    87–88, 93–94, 137
California State Teachers' Retirement
    System (CalSTRS), 57–58, 61, 88,
    108, 152
Call for Judgment, A (Bhidé), 32, 119
Cambridge Institute for Sustainability
    Leadership report (2015), 38
capital
    financial (governance), 87
    human (social), 87–88
    physical (environmental), 87
    social venture, 113
    See also value creation
capital market stability, 28–29
carbon dioxide (CO_2) emissions, 57
Carbon Efficiency Strategy, 161
Carney, Mark, 16
cash (asset class), 55, 67
Center on Budget and Policy Priorities,
    134–135
CEO compensation, 134, 135–136, 140–143
Ceres Investor Water Hub, 51
change. *See* climate change; systemic
    change
child labor, 98
chlorofluorocarbons, 34
Church of England Pensions Board,
    13–14, 80, 150, 153–154
Citigroup, 66
Cleaning Accountability Framework
    (Australia), 137
Climate Action 100+ project, 8, 36–37,
    57, 88, 154
Climate Action Plan (New York State
    Common Retirement Fund), 58
climate change
    applying a system-level lens to combat,
    7–9

Aviva Investors report (2014) made to
    UN on, 95
Climate Action 100+ project to reduce,
    36–37, 57, 154
current under reaction to, 23
economic consequences of, 1
fresh water resources reduced by, 51
how a sustainable investor might
    approach, 3
managers who successfully align others
    to address, 126
NBIM's expectations for companies
    regarding, 156
Paris Agreement on, 58, 125
relationship between ESG factors and
    risk of investment in, 87
"systemic risk" of, 46, 75
uncertainty and unpredictability of, 48
    See also environmental systems; ESG
    (environmental, social, and gover-
    nance) factors; greenhouse gases;
    systemic issues
Coalition for Environmentally
    Responsible Economies, 173
consensus criteria
    definition, importance, examples of
    issue, 49*t*
    as systemic issue, 43, 44
Construction and Building Unions
    Superannuation (Cbus), 105
consumer protection concerns (1970s), 97
conventional investing
    approach of, 2, 9
    bonds, 63
    investment tools of system-level vs., 74
    private equities, 59
    public equities, 56
    sovereign debt, 64
    transition to system-level from, 12–14
conventional investors
    advanced investment techniques sel-
    dom used by, 87
    description of, 2
    dismissal of ESG factors by, 2, 9
    investing focus of, 43
    investment beliefs of, 74–75
    manager selection and evaluation by, 82
    "Wall Street Walk" by dissatisfied, 78
corporate social responsibility (CSR),
    115, 116
corporations
    CEO compensation by, 134, 135–136,
    140–143
    corporate social responsibility (CSR),
    115, 116

corporations (*continued*)
  engaging them in systemic consider-
    ations, 78–81
  engaging them toward systemic change,
    58, 81
  fair treatment of employees by, 136–138
  "fissuring" workplace and, 133
  responsibility for taxes, 134–135
  stakeholder relations centered on ESG
    factors, 13
Corvair (General Motors), 97
Costco, 138
Council on Ethics (Norway), 98
Country Sustainability Ranking
  (RobecoSAM), 65
COVID-19 pandemic, 29, 129–130, 169
COVID bonds, 64
credit unions, 67

Dalio, Ray, 30
Daly, Herman, 28–29
dam collapse (Brazil), 79, 154
Dasra Social Impact, 92
Davis, Gardner, 30
Davis, Stephen, 33
Dialogue, 60
digital divide, 31
Diverse Director DataSource database, 88
diversity of approach technique
  investment enhancement by using the,
    89*f*, 100–102
  New Zealand Superannuation's applica-
    tion of, 149–150
"do no harm" investing approach, 96,
  98–99
due diligence, 113, 114–115, 127
Duke Energy, 57

economic growth
  CDPQ's mandated mission of promot-
    ing, 77–78
  IMF study findings on income inequal-
    ity and, 130
  impact of population growth on, 28
  importance of inclusive, 31
  water resources underpinning, 50
economy
  detrimental impact of income equality
    to, 130
  inequalities and disparities threat to
    stable, 1
  Japan's Government Pension
    Investment Fund "universal owners"
    of, 13, 151–152

effectiveness criteria
  definition, importance, examples of
    issue, 49*t*
  as systemic issue, 43, 46–47
Element AI, 60
employees
  corporate stakeholder relations and
    treatment of, 13
  ERAFP's compensation ratios between
    CEOs and their, 141–142
  fair treatment by corporations of their,
    136–138
  investing in youth, 157
  See also workplace
enterprise capital grants (Heron
  Foundation), 54
environmental activism (1960s), 97
environmental systems
  investing challenges of, 33–35
  paradigms of, 36*f*, 126
  "planetary boundaries" challenges, 34
  potential for instability of, 29–30
  short-term efficiency obsession and
    negative impact on, 33–34
  water resources underpinning sustain-
    ability of, 50
  See also climate change
equities
  private, 58–60
  public, 56–58
  security selection, 76–78
ESG (environmental, social, and governance) factors
  CalPERS's relating investment risk to,
    87, 94
  Cbus investment belief in, 105
  conventional investors' dismissal of,
    2, 9
  corporations' stakeholder relations
    centered on, 13
  manager selection and evaluation
    consideration of, 82–83
  Mercer's investment beliefs includ-
    ing, 75
  relationship between investor decisions
    and, 11
  SASB Materiality Map standards for
    corporate disclosure of, 27–28
  security selection/portfolio construc-
    tion consideration of, 76–78
  sustainable investors engaging compa-
    nies to improve their, 79
  sustainable investors' investing
    approach to, 2–3, 9, 26–28, 65
  system-level investing benefits for, 12–14

ESG (*continued*)
system-level investor focus on health
and stability of, 28–29
understanding importance of systems
to, 9–11
See also climate change; government;
healthcare system; societal systems
ESG integration
ESG Integration Framework (Allianz)
for, 158–159
McKnight Foundation's model for, 161
relationship between investor decisions
and, 11
system-level transition through, 158–159
three scenarios on system-level transition and, 162–166
ESG Risk Ratings framework
(Sustainalytics), 116
Établissement de retraite additionnelle
de la fonction publique (ERAFP),
141–142
Ethical Investor, The (Simon, Powers, and
Gunnemann), 160
European Union's green bonds taxonomy,
64
evaluating results
due diligence approach to, 113, 114–115,
127
major initiatives impacting measurement for, 115–117
Noyes Foundation's approach to, 113–114
principles and assumptions used in,
117–121
system-level investing step of, 18t, 20, 172
See also managers
evaluation assumptions
1. overall consistency of managers is
essential, 117–118
2. qualitative judgment/qualitative
metrics for decisions, 118–119
3. worth of social and environmental
systems, 119–120
4. balance is an ongoing investing challenge, 120–121
evaluation framework
the four assumptions of, 117–121
questions to ask, 122–126
evaluation questions
1. Are manager beliefs clear, actionable,
and adaptable?, 122
2. Can managers justify their choice of
systemic challenges?, 123
3. Have managers chosen investing techniques to create impact?,
123–124

4. Have managers leveraged the applied
techniques?, 124–125
5. Have managers' actions generated
desirable outcomes?, 125–126
6. How have managers contributed to
positive system shifts?, 126
evaluations technique
to generate investment opportunities,
89f, 104–105
reducing income inequality using the, 146
ExxonMobil, 160

fair labor practices, 87
Fair Work Ombudsman (Australia), 137
family office transition scenario, 164–165
F. B. Heron Foundation, 53–54, 58, 108
field-building techniques
description of, 89f
interconnectedness, 88, 89f, 93–94
polity, 88, 89f, 94–95, 146
self-organization, 88, 89f, 90–93,
145–146, 157
Fight for $15 minimum wage campaign
(UK), 138
financial capital (governance), 87
financial crisis (2008), 25–26, 32, 33, 119,
130
financial systems
COVID-19 pandemic impact on, 29
investing challenges of, 32–33
paradigms of, 36f, 126
potential for instability of, 29–30
scale and short-term profit taking challenges to, 32–33
Fissured Workplace, The (Weil), 133
fixed income, 55, 62
Florida State Board of Administration, 143
focus of investing. *See* investing focus
food security, 42–43, 157
Forestry and Agriculture Investment
Management, 157
fossil fuels, 34–35, 77, 160
fresh water resources
aquifers and glaciers, 51
criterion for system-level investment in
the, 50–51
investment tools applied to issue of,
83–85
leveraging advanced investment techniques applied to, 109, 110f
solutions approach to investing in, 99
system-level investment in the, 48
UN World Water Development Report
(2015) on, 50
See also systemic issues

Ganges River, 51
gender disparities, threat of, 1
General Motors (GM), 97
Georgia King Village (West Ward, Newark), 70
Gini Index, 131
glaciers and aquifers, 51
global financial crisis (2008), 25–26, 32, 33, 119, 130
Global Impact Investing Network (GIIN), 92, 156
Global Investor Coalition on Climate Change, 36–37
Global Reporting Initiative, 115
Global Stewardship Principles (ICGN), 153
goals
    conventional investors' focus on maximizing returns, 24–26
    sustainable investors' focus on social/environmental, 26–28
    UN Sustainable Development Goals (SDGs), 27, 35, 36, 44, 61, 95, 114, 157
    See also system-level goals
Goldman Sachs, 66
government
    governance as financial capital, 87
    investor collaboration with NGOs and, 42, 46–47, 51
    need for increased role in financial system by, 33
    phenomenon of populism impact on stability of, 30–31
    See also ESG (environmental, social, and governance) factors
Government Pension Fund Global (NBIM), 155
Government Pension Investment Fund (GPIF; Japan), 13, 150, 151–152
Grantham, Mayo, Van Otterloo & Co., 134
Great Recession (2008), 25–26, 32, 33, 119, 130
"green bonds," 63–64
Green Bond Standards Working Group, 64
greenhouse gases
    carbon dioxide (CO_2) emissions, 57
    chlorofluorocarbons causing, 34
    Climate Action 100+ project to reduce, 36–37, 57, 154
    fossil fuels creating, 33–35, 77, 160
    See also climate change

Hadarim Fund, 93
Hahne renovation (Newark), 69

Harvard Business Review, 138
Hawley, James, 10
healthcare system
    Access to Medicine Index on inequalities of, 31
    corporations' stakeholder relations centered on, 13
    human capital concerns of health and safety, 87
    system-level lens to improve, 5–7
    See also ESG (environmental, social, and governance) factors
HeidelbergCement, 37
Hermes Investment Management (Hermes EOS), 80–81
Heron Foundation, 53–54, 58, 108
Hope Credit Union (Mississippi), 67
HSBC Global Asset Management, 37
human capital, 87–88
Human Capital Management Coalition, 88
Human Development Index (United Nations), 44
human rights, 13, 81, 156, 160

Ilmarinen (Finland), 140
ImpactAssets, 92
impact investing
    KL Felicitas Foundation's commitment to, 14, 91–92, 150
    system-level transition to, 156–157
Impact Management Project, 117
income inequality
    applying lessons to reducing system-level, 143–146
    CEO compensation contributing to, 134, 135–136, 140–143
    corporations' stakeholder relations centered on, 13
    detrimental impact to society and economy by, 130
    encouraging appropriate taxation to reduce, 138–140
    the "fissuring" workplace contributes to, 133
    improving labor relations to reduce, 136–138
    labor relations and reducing, 136–138
    Lakner and Milanovic's study of global (1988–2008), 131
    the paradigm shift required for reducing, 135–136
    relevance to investments by, 45–46
    system-level investment approach to, 4–5, 20–21

income inequality (*continued*)
2016 report on investor contributions
to, 132
understanding the global threat of, 1
See also inequalities
Indus River, 51
inequalities
corporations' stakeholder relations
centered on, 13
healthcare access, 31
racial, 1
social, 4–5, 30–32
as societal threat, 1
system-level investment approach to
diminish, 4–5, 20–21
See also income inequality
infrastructure
asset class of, 55, 69–70
manager promotion of system-related
change, 125–126
responsible contractor policies (RCPs)
for investing in, 137
Innovest, 116
instability
COVID-19 pandemic causing, 29
investing to prevent system, 29–30
phenomenon of populism causing, 30–31
Institutional Investors Group on Climate
Change, 154
interconnectedness technique, 88, 89f,
93–94
International Capital Market Association's
Green Bond Principles, 64
International Corporate Governance
Network (ICGN), 153
International Finance Corporation (IFC),
116
International Integrated Reporting
Council (IIRC), 105
International Monetary Fund (IMF), 130
investing focus
of conventional investors, 43
how to measure a system-level, 42–43
of system-level investors, 17t, 19, 41–52,
170
investment beliefs
of CalPERS relating risk to ESG factors,
75, 87, 94
of Cbus in ESG factors, 105
conventional investors and, 74–75
evaluating results by asking about
manager's, 122
investment beliefs statement (IBS), 74,
76, 122
Mercer, 75

sustainable investors and, 75
Washington State Investment Board
(WSIB), 76
investment beliefs statement (IBS)
description and use of, 74, 76
evaluating results by asking about, 122
Washington State Investment Board
(WSIB), 76
investment-enhancement techniques
description of, 89f, 95–96
diversity of approach, 89f, 100–102,
149–150
solutions, 89f, 98–100
standards setting, 89f, 96–98, 159–161
investment returns
balance between strengthening systems
and, 146–147
conventional investing goal of maximizing, 24–26
developing a long-term view of, 32
impact of system stability on, 10–11
"market beta" swings and, 11
modern portfolio theory (MPT) on risk
and, 11, 24–25
relevance of income inequality to,
45–46
sustainable investing goal on social,
environmental, and, 26–28
system-level investing goal on health,
stability, and, 28–29
21st century destabilizing challenges
to, 1–2
investment tools
applied to fresh water issue, 83–85
applied to reduce income inequality,
144–145
comparing conventional to system-level
use of, 74
engaging corporations on systemic considerations, 78–81
investment beliefs statement (IBS),
74, 76
leveraging advanced techniques, 18t,
20, 87–111, 171
manager selection and evaluation,
82–83, 122–126
security selection and portfolio construction, 76–78
system-level application of, 18t, 20,
71–85
investor decisions
ESG considerations of sustainable, 2–3,
9, 26–28
financial crisis (2008) driven by mechanized, 119

investor decisions (*continued*)
  global financial crisis (2008) and role
    of, 25–26
  relationship between ESG and, 11
  See also managers
investors
  conventional, 2, 9, 43, 74–75, 78, 82, 87
  sustainable, 2–3, 9, 26–28, 65, 75, 79,
    82, 87
  2016 report on contributions to income
    inequality by, 132
  See also managers; system-level
    investors
Ircantec, 37
Ireland Strategic Investment Fund (ISIF),
  106–107
IRIS+, 116
Ivanhoé Cambridge, 78

Japan's Government Pension Investment
  Fund (GPIF), 13, 150, 151–152
Jessie Smith Noyes Foundation, 113–114
Jobs, Steve, 91
JPMorgan Chase, 66

Keynes, John Maynard, 47
KLD Research & Analytics, 116
Kleissner, Charly, 91, 157, 166
Kleissner, Lisa, 91, 157, 166
KL Felicitas Foundation, 14, 91–92, 150,
  156–157
Krugman, Paul, 144
Kryger, Steven, 30

labor standards
  reducing income inequality with
    higher, 136–138
  responsible contractor policies (RCPs)
    setting, 137
Lakner, Christoph, 131
LEED (Leadership in Energy and
  Environmental Design) certified
  assets, 61
leveraging advanced techniques. *See*
  advanced investment techniques
Living Forests, 157
loans, 55, 62, 65–67
Local Authority Pension Fund Forum
  (UK), 140
locality technique, 89*f*, 106–107
"Long Hot Summer of 1967" race riots, 71
Longroad Energy Holdings, 102
low-carbon Index (LCI), 57
Lukomnik, Jon, 10, 33
Lydenberg, Steve, 15

Maersk, 37
managers
  due diligence when assessing ability of,
    113, 114–115, 127
  implementing equitable pay for, 136
  principles and assumptions about,
    117–121
  questions to ask when evaluating,
    122–126
  selection and evaluation of, 82–83,
    122–126
  See also evaluating results; investor
    decisions; investors
Manulife Investment Management, 37
MA'O Organic Farms (Hawaii), 157
"market beta" swings, 11
Marsh & McLennan Companies, 75
Massachusetts Institute of Technology, 124
Massie, Bob, 173
McDonald's, 138
McKnight Foundation, 161
Meadows, Donella, 124
Mekong River, 51
Mellon Capital Management, 161
Mercer (Marsh & McLennan Companies),
  75
Methodist church, 96
microfinancing, 31
Milanovic, Branko, 131
Military Park (Newark), 70
modern portfolio theory (MPT)
  extending stock analysis to portfolios, 9
  on managing risk and return, 11, 24–25
modern slavery, 81
Montreal Protocol (1987), 34
Moody's, 116
Morgan Stanley, 66
Morningstar, 116
mortgages (questionable), 32
MSCI, 116

Nader, Ralph, 97
National Intelligence Council, 12–13
NEET (not in education, employment, or
  training), 104
Nestlé, 37
Newark (New Jersey)
  infrastructure investment in, 69–70
  Prudential Global Investment
    Management (PGIM)'s PII invest-
    ment in, 72–73
  race riots (1967) in, 71
New Jersey Performing Arts Center
  (Newark), 70

New York State Common Retirement
Fund
Climate Action Plan, 58
formal RCPs used by, 137
Sustainable Investment and Climate
Solutions Program, 58
New Zealand Gourmet, 102
New Zealand Superannuation (NZ
Super), 100–102, 149–150
NeXT Computer, 91
NGOs (nongovernmental organizations)
IIRC coalition including, 105
investor collaboration on health issues
with, 46–47
investor collaboration with government
and, 42, 51
World Wildlife Fund, 95
Nordea Group, 64
Norges Bank Investment Management
(NBIM), 13, 98, 139–140, 150,
155–156, 166
Noyes Foundation, 113–114
nuclear safety, 99, 160

ocean sustainability, 156
Operating Principles for Impact
Management (IFC), 116
opportunity-generation techniques
additionality, 89f, 102–104
description of, 89f, 102
evaluations, 89f, 104–105, 146
locality, 89f, 106–107
utility, 89f, 107–109
Organization for Economic Co-operation
and Development (OECD)
Better Life Index of the, 44
standard-setting initiative of, 98
Otéra Capital, 78
"Our Partnership for Sustainable Capital
Markets," 152
ownership
Japan's Government Pension
Investment Fund approach to, 13,
151–152
"Our Partnership for Sustainable
Capital Markets" on universal, 152
practice of stewardship and concept
of, 13–14
See also stewardship
ozone layer, 34–35

pandemics
COVID-19, 29, 64, 129–130
economic consequences of, 129–130

paradigms
societal, financial, environmental, 36f
system-level, 35–36
paradigm shifts
CEO compensation issue, 140–143
encouraging appropriate taxation, 139
evaluating how managers contributed
positive, 126
reducing income inequality requires a,
135–136
required for achieving SDGs, 36
required for system-level goals, 37–38
Paris Agreement, 58, 125
partnership goals (SDGs), 27
Patton, Michael Quinn, 117
peace goals (SDGs), 27
pension funds
AP pension funds' Council on Ethics,
79–80
Church of England Pensions Board,
13–14, 80, 150, 153–154
Government Pension Fund Global
(NBIM), 155
Japan's Government Pension
Investment Fund (GPIF), 13, 150,
151–152
Local Authority Pension Fund Forum
(UK), 140
system-level transition scenario on
large, 162–163
USS Investment Management, 152
people goals (SDGs), 27
PGGM, 99
physical capital (environmental), 87
Pitt-Watson, David, 33
planet goals (SDGs), 27
polity technique
to build system-level influence, 146
field-building using the, 88, 89f, 94–95
pollution
carbon dioxide (CO$_2$) emissions, 57
chlorofluorocarbons, 34
Climate Action 100+ project to reduce,
36–37, 57, 154
fossil fuels consumption and, 34–35, 77
population growth, 28
populism phenomenon, 30–31
portfolio management
comparing manager performance
discipline of, 114–115
conventional single solution approach
to, 100
Noyes Foundation systemic change
approach to, 113–114

portfolios
constructed to reduce income inequality, 145
emphasizing system fortifiers in construction of, 76–78
targeted toward solving ESG problems,
14
See also asset classes
poverty
as systemic issue, 44
water resources underpinning reduction of, 50
*Practical Guide to ESG Integration for
Equity Investing, A* (PRI), 158
PricewaterhouseCoopers study, 120
principles-focused evaluation, 117–121
Principles for Responsible Banking,
66–67
Principles for Responsible Investment
(PRI), 82, 132, 158
private equities, 55, 58–60
private equity firm transition scenario,
165–166
problem solving
solutions investing technique, 89f,
98–100
Tolstoy's *The Big Oven* on settling for
short-term, 23
Project Ireland 2040, 107
prosperity goals (SDGs), 27
Prudential Financial, 69, 71–72
Prudential Global Investment
Management (PGIM), 69, 72–73, 109
Prudential Impact Investments (PII) unit,
72–73
Public Citizen, 97
public equities, 55, 56–58

Qatar operations (Hermes), 81

race riots (1967), 71
racial inequality, 1
real assets
infrastructure, 55, 69–70
real estate, 55, 67–69
real estate, 55, 67–69
relevance criteria
definition, importance, examples of
issue, 49t
as systemic issue, 43, 45–46
resources. *See* asset resources
responsible contractor policies (RCPs),
137
returns. *See* investment returns
Rio Tinto, 37

Rise of Fiduciary Capitalism, The (Hawley
and Williams), 152
risks
CalPERS investment belief on relating
ESG factors to, 87, 94
climate change as a "systemic," 46, 75
modern portfolio theory (MPT) on
returns and, 11, 24–25
WSIB's investment beliefs statement on
systemic global, 76
RobecoSAM's Country Sustainability
Ranking, 65
"robosigning" practice, 32
Rockefeller Brothers Fund, 77, 150,
160–161
Rockefeller, John D., 160
Rogers, Jason, 30
Rwanda farmers, 157

Sam's Club, 138
S&P ESG Sovereign Bond Index Family,
65
SDGs (United Nations Sustainable
Development Goals), 27
Securities and Exchange Commission
(SEC), 132
security selection, 76–78
Self-Help Credit Union (North Carolina),
67
Self-Help Enterprises (SHE), 53–54
self-organization technique
field-building using the, 88, 89f, 90–93,
157
reducing income inequality using the,
145–146
setting goals. *See* system-level goals
SIRI (Sustainable Investment Research
Initiative) Library (CalPERS), 93–94
slavery, 81
SMART framework, 116
"social" bonds, 64
social inequities
corporate trends driving, 30–32
phenomenon of populism and, 30–31
system-level investment approach to
diminish, 4–5
social justice movements (1960s), 97
social venture capital, 113
societal systems
corporate trends, social inequities, and
crisis of, 30–32
COVID-19 pandemic impact on, 29
paradigms of, 36f, 126
phenomenon of populism and instabilities of, 30–31

societal systems (*continued*)
  potential for instability of, 29–30
  See also ESG (environmental, social,
    and governance) factors
society
  detrimental impact of income equality
    to, 130
  inequalities and disparities threat to
    cohesive, 1
  system-level investor focus on health
    and stability of, 28–29
solutions technique, 89*f*, 98–100
Sonen Capital, 92
South African apartheid, 97–98, 160
Southern Bancorp, 67
sovereign debt, 55, 64–65
sovereign development fund, 106–107
sovereign wealth funds, 106
Standard Oil Company, 160
standards setting
  definition in context of investing, 159
  as investment-enhancement technique,
    89*f*, 96–98
  system-level transition through,
    159–161
stewardship
  Church of England Pensions Board
    embrace of, 153–154
  definition of, 153
  International Corporate Governance
    Network, 153
  investors' ownership and practice of,
    13–14
  Mercer's investment belief in, 75
  system-level investors taking, 38–39
  See also ownership
Stewardship Implementation Framework
  (Church of England Pensions Board),
  153
Stiglitz, Joseph, 144
Stockholm Resilience Centre (SRC), 34
Sullivan Principles, 97–98
Sullivan, Reverend Leon, 97
Sustainability Accounting Standards
  Board (SASB), 27, 46, 115–116
Sustainable Development Goals (SDGs;
  UN), 27, 35, 36, 44, 61, 95, 114, 157
sustainable investing
  approach of, 2–3, 9
  bonds, 63
  private equities, 59
  public equities, 56
  sovereign debt, 64–65
  transition to system-level from, 12–14
  venture capital, 61

Sustainable Investment and Climate
  Solutions Program (New York State
  Common Retirement Fund), 58
Sustainable Investment Research
  Initiative (SIRI) Library (CalPERS),
  93–94
sustainable investors
  advanced investment techniques sel-
    dom used by, 87
  description of, 2–3
  engaging corporations on systemic con-
    siderations, 79
  ESG considerations by, 2–3, 9, 26–28, 65
  financial materiality of ESG factors
    considered by, 2–3, 9
  investment beliefs of, 75
  manager selection and evaluation by, 82
  SDGs framework used by, 27–28
Sustainalytics, 116
Sydney Metro mass-transit system, 60
systemic change
  applying lessons to reduce income
    equality, 143–146
  asset classes used to create, 54–55
  as a clear and possible reality, 172–173
  engaging corporations toward, 58, 81
  Noyes Foundation's intention to create,
    113–114
  utility technique to create, 108–109
systemic issue criteria
  1. consensus, 43, 44, 49*t*
  2. relevance, 43, 45–46, 49*t*
  3. effectiveness, 43, 46–47, 49*t*
  4. uncertainty, 43, 47–48, 49*t*
systemic issues
  criteria of, 43–51
  food security, 42–43, 157
  human rights, 13, 81, 156, 160
  taking the first steps toward adopt-
    ing, 52
  See also climate change; fresh water
    resources
systemic risks
  climate change understood as a, 46, 75
  security selection/portfolio construc-
    tion consideration of, 76–78
  WSIB's investment beliefs statement on
    global, 76
system-level goals
  for environmental systems, 33–35
  for financial systems, 32–33
  focused on system-level paradigms,
    35–36, 36*f*, 126
  paradigm shifts required for investing
    with, 37–38, 126

system-level goals (*continued*)
  to reduce income equality, 144–145
  required for system-level investing, 17*t*,
    19, 23–39, 170
  thinking systemically to set and
    achieve, 38–39
  See also goals
system-level influence
  adopting techniques designed for,
    145–146
  evaluation technique to build, 146
  polity technique to build, 146
  self-organization technique to build,
    145–146
system-level investing
  benefits for ESG factors by, 12
  bonds, 63–64
  introduction to the process of, 17–21, 17*t*
  private equity, 59–60
  public equities, 57
  TIIP's work to helping institutional
    investors with, 15–16, 88
  the transition from convention and
    sustainable to, 12–14
  understanding the importance of
    systems to markets, 9–11
  venture capital, 61
  why the time to act is now, 169–170
system-level investing steps
  1. set goals, 17*t*, 19, 23–39, 170
  2. decide where to focus, 17*t*, 19, 41–52,
    170
  3. allocate assets, 17*t*, 19–20, 53–70, 171
  4. apply investment tools, 18*t*, 20,
    71–85, 171
  5. leverage advanced techniques, 18*t*,
    20, 87–111, 171–172
  6. evaluate results, 18*t*, 20, 113–127, 172
system-level investors
  approach to ESG factors by, 4–9
  collaboration with government and
    NGOs by, 42, 46–47, 51
  description of, 3–4
  engaging corporations on systemic con-
    siderations, 79–81
  health and stability focus of, 28–29
  investing focus of, 17*t*, 19, 41–52, 170
  learning to think systemically, 38–39
  See also investors
system-level transition
  Allianz, 142–143, 150, 158–159
  Church of England Pensions Board,
    13–14, 80, 150, 153–154
  examining six investors making the,
    150–151

Global Impact Investing Network
    (GIIN), 92, 156
Japan's Government Pension
    Investment Fund (GPIF), 13, 150,
    151–152
KL Felicitas Foundation, 14, 91–92, 150,
    156–157
MA'O Organic Farms, 157
McKnight Foundation, 161
moving toward the, 12–14
New Zealand Superannuation, 149–150
Norges Bank Investment Management
    (NBIM), 13, 98, 139–140, 150,
    155–156, 166
Rockefeller Brothers Fund, 77, 150,
    160–161
taking the first steps toward, 166–167
system-level transition scenarios
  1. large pension fund, 162–163
  2. family office, 164–165
  3. private equity firm, 165–166
system-level transition steps
  1. universal ownership, 151–152
  2. stewardship, 153–154
  3. long-term value creation, 154–156
  4. impact investing, 156–157
  5. ESG integration, 158–159
  6. standards setting, 159–161
systems
  health and stability of, 28–29
  impact on health of markets by, 10
  potential instability of social, financial,
    and environmental, 29–30
  system-level goals focused on para-
    digms of, 35–36, 36*f*, 126
  taking stewardship responsibility for,
    13–14, 38–39
  understanding importance to markets
    by, 9–11
  See also ESG (environmental, social,
    and governance) factors

T100 project (Toniic Tracer), 92
tailing pond dam collapse (Brazil), 79, 154
Talent.com, 60
Task Force on Climate-Related Financial
    Disclosures, 81
taxation
  corporate tax transparency, 156
  income inequality and corporate avoid-
    ance of, 134–135
  reducing income inequality with appro-
    priate, 138–140
Thinking in Systems (Meadows), 124

TIIP (The Investment Integration
  Project), 15–16, 88
Tolstoy, Leo, 23
Toniic, 92–93
Toniic Tracer platform, 92
Ton, Zeynep, 138
Total Impact Capital, 92
Trader Joe's, 138
"tragedy of the commons," 93
transitioning process. *See* system-level
  transition
21st century investing. *See* system-level
  investing

uncertainty criteria
  climate change unpredictability and, 48
  definition, importance, examples of
    issue, 49*t*
  as systemic issue, 43, 47–48
United Kingdom
  Bank of England, 16
  Church of England Pensions Board,
    13–14, 80, 150, 153–154
  Fight for $15 minimum wage campaign,
    138
  Local Authority Pension Fund Forum,
    140
  USS Investment Management pension
    fund, 152
United Nations
  Aviva Investors climate change report
    (2014) made to, 95
  Environment Programme Finance
    Initiative (2019), 66
  Human Development Index, 44
  Principles for Responsible Investment
    (PRI), 82, 132, 158
  Sustainable Development Goals
    (SDGs), 27, 35, 36, 44, 61, 95, 114, 157
  World Water Development Report
    (2015), 50
universal ownership concept, 13, 151–152
Unsafe at Any Speed (Nader), 97
urban renewal initiatives, 69–70
US Community Investing Index (USCII;
  Heron Foundation), 54
USS Investment Management pension
  fund (UK), 152
utility technique, 89*f*, 107–109

Vale (mining company), 79–80, 154
value creation
  corporate tax avoidance to increase,
    134–135
  moving beyond capital to long-term,
    105
  system-level transition requiring long-
    term, 154–156
  tradeoff between short-term and long-
    term, 121
  See also capital
venture capital, 55, 61
Vert Asset Management, 68
Vigeo Eiris, 116
Volkswagen, 37

"Wall Street Walk," 78
Walmart, 138
Washington State Investment Board
  (WSIB), 76
water resources. *See* fresh water resources
World Water Development Report (2015;
  UN), 50
Waygood, Steve, 95
wealth inequality. *See* income inequality
Weil, David, 133
Wells Fargo, 66
Wesley, John, 96
What They Do with Your Money (Davis,
  Lukomnik, and Pitt-Watson), 33
Workforce Disclosure Initiative (WDI),
  136
workplace
  the "fissuring," 133
  stakeholder concerns over conditions
    in the, 13
  See also employees
World Wildlife Fund, 95

Xcel Energy, 37

Yangtze River, 51
youth employment, 157

About the Authors

William Burckart

 For nearly twenty years William Burckart has explored how private capital can be used to change the world. Whether researching, writing, consulting with clients, or gesticulating wildly at podiums, he seeks to engage people who want to leverage the tools of finance for change.

William is the first to admit this field he has chosen is not well defined—he often describes it as the "island of misfit toys" from the 1964 classic *Rudolph the Red-Nosed Reindeer*. William is certainly a misfit toy himself, with degrees in policy, economics, and international affairs from George Washington University and Johns Hopkins University. His graduate work focused on how young venture capitalists from the dot-com boom era changed philanthropy. This led to a stint supporting impact performance analysis for Venture Philanthropy Partners (VPP).

At VPP, William was introduced to the discipline of systems dynamics and the pioneering work of Donella Meadows. The desire to learn more about systems pulled him back into research, allowing him to work on *New Frontiers of Philanthropy: A Guide to the New Tools and Actors Reshaping Global Philanthropy and Social Investing*. The book explored the edges of philanthropy and social investing and provided insights into this new era of social-purpose finance.

Itching to once again play on the island of misfit toys rather than just research it, William returned to consulting and applied research, founding or cofounding a series of impact investing practices, and, in partnership with Steve Lydenberg, ultimately helped establish The Investment Integration Project (TIIP). He began working with investment management firms, private foundations, government, and major industry bodies to develop and implement big-picture investment strategies that consider systemic impact.

Along the way, he has served as a visiting scholar to the US Federal Reserve Bank of San Francisco, as a fellow with the High Meadows Institute, and as a member of the advisory council of the Investments & Wealth Institute's WealthBoard 100. He has also tormented graduate students with his guest lectures on sustainable investing at Columbia University, Georgetown University, and New York University.

His writing has been featured or covered by the *Guardian*, *Forbes*, *Quartz*, *Stanford Social Innovation Review*, *ImpactAlpha*, *CSRwire*, *Alliance*, and the *Chronicle of Philanthropy* and at the first G8-level forum on impact investing. He has presented at the US Federal Reserve, the Money Management Institute, the Morningstar Sustainable Investment Forum, PRI in Person, the GIIN Investor Forum, and CFA Institute, to name a few.

He splits his time between San Diego and New York City.

Steve Lydenberg

Over the past four decades, Steve Lydenberg has had a ringside seat from which to follow the development of sustainable investment and corporate social responsibility (CSR) as they have evolved from curiosities to mainstream trends.

For twelve years, starting in the mid-1970s, he conducted research for the Council on Economic Priorities, which was among the first US organizations to rate and rank corporations on their social and environmental records. He made the shift over to the investment community in 1987, when he joined Franklin Research & Development Corporation—now Trillium Asset Management—one of the first pure-play sustainable investment money managers. Then in 1990 he joined Amy Domini and Peter Kinder in the founding of KLD Research & Analytics, one of the first firms devoted primarily to sustainable investment research. While there, he played key roles in the development of KLD's database of the CSR profiles of the largest publicly traded US corporations—a first of its kind—and the creation of the first socially screened broad-market stock index.

In 2001, he joined Domini Impact Investments, a mutual fund company specializing in sustainable and impact investment funds, as CIO and currently holds the position of partner, strategic vision. Sensing the need for a nonprofit organization to conduct fundamental research in the rapidly growing sustainable investment field, he founded the Initiative for Responsible

Investment, currently housed at the Hauser Institute for Civil Society at the Harvard Kennedy School.

Believing that the investment community was approaching a tipping point by 2015 at which fundamental change was possible, Steve founded TIIP with William Burckart. Since then, TIIP has promoted the next steps it views as essential for the evolution of investment: incorporation of social and environmental systemic risks and rewards into the sustainable investment process to bring fundamental change to the operating principles of investment.

Along the way Steve has authored and coauthored five books on sustainable investment and corporate social responsibility, including *Corporations and the Public Interest: Guiding the Invisible Hand,* and published numerous book chapters, monographs, and articles in journals, including the *Journal of Business Ethics, Journal of Corporate Citizenship,* and *Journal of Applied Corporate Finance.* Steve is a CFA charter holder and lives in Brooklyn with his wife, Robin.

Berrett–Koehler
Publishers

Berrett-Koehler is an independent publisher dedicated to an ambitious mission: *Connecting people and ideas to create a world that works for all.*

Our publications span many formats, including print, digital, audio, and video. We also offer online resources, training, and gatherings. And we will continue expanding our products and services to advance our mission.

We believe that the solutions to the world's problems will come from all of us, working at all levels: in our society, in our organizations, and in our own lives. Our publications and resources offer pathways to creating a more just, equitable, and sustainable society. They help people make their organizations more humane, democratic, diverse, and effective (and we don't think there's any contradiction there). And they guide people in creating positive change in their own lives and aligning their personal practices with their aspirations for a better world.

And we strive to practice what we preach through what we call "The BK Way." At the core of this approach is *stewardship,* a deep sense of responsibility to administer the company for the benefit of all of our stakeholder groups, including authors, customers, employees, investors, service providers, sales partners, and the communities and environment around us. Everything we do is built around stewardship and our other core values of *quality, partnership, inclusion,* and *sustainability.*

This is why Berrett-Koehler is the first book publishing company to be both a B Corporation (a rigorous certification) and a benefit corporation (a for-profit legal status), which together require us to adhere to the highest standards for corporate, social, and environmental performance. And it is why we have instituted many pioneering practices (which you can learn about at www.bkconnection.com), including the Berrett-Koehler Constitution, the Bill of Rights and Responsibilities for BK Authors, and our unique Author Days.

We are grateful to our readers, authors, and other friends who are supporting our mission. We ask you to share with us examples of how BK publications and resources are making a difference in your lives, organizations, and communities at www.bkconnection.com/impact.

Dear reader,

Thank you for picking up this book and welcome to the worldwide BK community! You're joining a special group of people who have come together to create positive change in their lives, organizations, and communities.

What's BK all about?

Our mission is to connect people and ideas to create a world that works for all.

Why? Our communities, organizations, and lives get bogged down by old paradigms of self-interest, exclusion, hierarchy, and privilege. But we believe that can change. That's why we seek the leading experts on these challenges—and share their actionable ideas with you.

A welcome gift

To help you get started, we'd like to offer you a **free copy** of one of our bestselling ebooks:

www.bkconnection.com/welcome

When you claim your **free ebook**, you'll also be subscribed to our blog.

Our freshest insights

Access the best new tools and ideas for leaders at all levels on our blog at ideas.bkconnection.com.

Sincerely,

Your friends at Berrett-Koehler

Certified

Corporation